According to His Kind Intention

A Collection of Inspirational Writings

According to His Kind Intention

A Collection of Inspirational Writings

Denese S. Brown

ACCORDING TO HIS KIND INTENTION
by Denese S. Brown
Revised Edition

Copyright © 2024 Denese S. Brown
All rights reserved

All rights reserved. This book is protected under the copyright laws of the United States of America. No portion of this book may be reproduced in any form, without the written permission of the publisher. Permission granted on request.

ISBN: 979-8-9875001-9-4

Unless otherwise indicated, Scripture taken from the New King James Version®. Copyright © 1982 by Thomas Nelson. Used by permission. All rights reserved.

Design Director: Dawn Harvey-Owens

Published by:
UPH. Div., Maximized Productions Publishing Division
6715 Suitland Road
Morningside, Maryland 20746
(701)484-3303
www.maximizedproductions.com/publishing/

Printed in the USA

Table of Contents

ACKNOWLEDGEMENTS 8
PREFACE 9
Foundational Scriptures 11
HIS LOVE 13
His Love 14
His Mercy 16
His Presence 20
His Rest 22
His Word 26
WALKING WITH GOD 28
God Has a Plan 29
Worship the Lord 32
Our Provider 36
Grace Apprehended 38
The River of Giving 43
A Journey with Fears and Faith 45
A Scene from Heaven! 48
SPIRITUAL FRUIT 49
Sweet Fruit 50
Anger, Healing, and Forgiveness 54
Bitterness and Grace 59
Joy in Trials 62
LIFE LESSONS 67
Remember the Basics 68
Don't be Discouraged! 72
Rhythms of Grace 75

Forgiveness	77
Be Available	80
Giving...God Said Test Me!	84
Rest in the Power of God	87
JESUS	92
I AM With You	93
Jesus - The Christ	96
Let this Mind Be In You	97
The Great "I AM"	100
Our Faith	102
God's Rest is a Gift	105
The Beginning of Wisdom	109
True Riches	113
Truth That Transforms	116
A Message for Life	120
My Confession	126
PRAYER	128
Resist Evil - Warfare is Essential	129
What Hinders Our Prayers?	135
We Must Pray	139
Prayer Against Double-Mindedness	143
Prayer for Help	144
Prayer of Confession	145
Prayer of Thankfulness and Blessings	146
Prayer of Trust and Thankfulness	147
Prayer: Spiritual Weapons	148
Yes, Lord!	150
Quotes from Other Faith Leaders:	151

A Message on Joy 151
Prayer In Closing... 157
About the Author 159
References 161

ACKNOWLEDGEMENTS

To my mother, Pearl, who hopes for God's best in her children.

To my husband, Roger, who is my loving life partner and champion.

To my friend, Dawn, who was sent as a gift from God. I am forever grateful for you.

And finally, to my son, LaMar, who gave me much material for this book.

PREFACE

Only God can give rest for your soul, peace in hard times, and hope amidst disappointments. Only He can heal a broken heart, give power to forgive, and set us free from burdens and bitter failures in this fallen world-most importantly, give us eternal life through faith in Jesus Christ.

This book was written to reflect His desire to commune with us as we experience His lovingkindness. The essence of His presence and the power of His truth will answer all of our questions, address our struggles, and fulfill the joys of life.
So often, when difficulties arise, we turn to family, friends, and loved ones, but God wants us to turn to Him first! God wants us to deal with our challenges and disappointments as we seek His face and trust that He only means us well and His Intentions are kind.

Walking in His abiding love will impact how we live, make decisions, and respond to God and others. It is only when we decide (an act of our will) to believe with our whole heart that God sincerely loves us and we embrace the deep reservoir of His love that we can then understand His expansive love, experience His abiding presence, and have the confident peace of knowing Him. We have revised the original book to include new devotionals and updated words of encouragement.

It is my prayer that this book accomplishes His divine intention towards you as a transformative expression of intimate communion with the Father and His Son, Jesus Christ.

Foundational Scriptures

Ephesians 1:3-9
³ All praise to God, the Father of our Lord Jesus Christ, who has blessed us with every spiritual blessing in the heavenly realms because we are united with Christ. ⁴ Even before he made the world, God loved us and chose us in Christ to be holy and without fault in his eyes. ⁵ God decided in advance to adopt us into his own family by bringing us to himself through Jesus Christ. This is what he wanted to do, and it gave him great pleasure. ⁶ So we praise God for the glorious grace he has poured out on us who belong to his dear Son. ⁷ He is so rich in kindness and grace that he purchased our freedom with the blood of his Son and forgave our sins. ⁸ He has showered his kindness on us, along with all wisdom and understanding.

Ephesian 3:14-19
¹⁴ When I think of all this, I fall to my knees and pray to the Father, ¹⁵ the Creator of everything in heaven and on earth. ¹⁶ I pray that from his glorious, unlimited resources he will empower you with inner strength through his Spirit. ¹⁷ Then Christ will make his home in your hearts as you trust in him. Your roots will grow down into God's love and keep you strong. ¹⁸ And may you have the power to understand, as all God's people should, how wide, how long, how high, and how deep his love is. ¹⁹ May you experience the love of Christ, though it is too great to understand fully. Then you will be made complete with all the fullness of life and power that comes from God. NLT

2 Corinthians 12:8-10

⁸ Three different times I begged the Lord to take it away. ⁹ Each time he said, "My grace is all you need. My power works best in weakness." So now I am glad to boast about my weaknesses, so that the power of Christ can work through me. ¹⁰ That's why I take pleasure in my weaknesses, and in the insults, hardships, persecutions, and troubles that I suffer for Christ. For when I am weak, then I am strong.

Isaiah 43:2

When you go through deep waters, I will be with you. When you go through rivers of difficulty, you will not drown. When you walk through the fire of oppression, you will not be burned up; the flames will not consume you.

HIS LOVE

His Love

Gives all, suffers long, covers shame, redeems souls, waits patiently, forgives sin, and not selfish. Has no fear, carries us through, rejoices in truth, better than life

And remains forever…When love is disappointed, wounded, and frustrated, it perseveres; it suffers long.[i]

Love carries us during hard times, knowing that hope glimmers in darkness. Love hopes for the best and cleans up our mess. Love challenges faults and encourages our strengths. At its best, love covers our many frailties and sins. Love forgives over and over and over again...

Love looks to God for help, for God is love.[ii]

Even when abandoned, love prays for you and with you, only wanting God's best. Love is obligated - it must sacrifice and love the unlovely.
Love hurts so "good"-Quietly, it grows deeper and surprises you with joy and laughter.

Love speaks the truth with kindness.
Love is discreet (it will not expose your shame).
Love is loyal, grateful, and considerate. With its passion for commitment, love stays. The essence of love is eternal.

Love is courageous; it fights, serves, and pays the cost to remain-As time passes, sweetness blossoms-yes, a sweet aroma that transforms relationships.

There is no greater example of love than this-while we were still in our sins, Jesus Christ died! At the moment of our greatest need, He loved us best....[iii]

"Above all, keep fervent in your love for one another, because love covers a multitude of sins."[iv]

His Mercy

"...Mercy triumphs over judgment" (James 2:13)

"Mercy triumphs over judgment." The word mercy means compassion. God declares, "I want My people to know who I Am." He is the only true and living God. And He is God who says, "My mercy is new every morning" (Lamentations 3:21-26). Every morning that we awake, His mercy is available to us. We had enough for yesterday and today and will have enough for tomorrow. Compassion-God says, "I'm faithful and my mercy is new every morning. Great is thy faithfulness" (Lamentations 3:21-26). The Book of James is the Wisdom Book of the New Testament. And when you read the book of James, the first chapter states that if you lack wisdom, go to God; He is generous with wisdom. (James 1:5).

In Chapter 2 of James, the writer goes on to talk about why it's so important not to be prejudiced, biased, or treat people you may feel are important better than others-the key reason is that Jesus died for every human being. God showed how much He valued all of us when He gave His Life as a ransom. The moment God decided to send Jesus to pay the price for our sins is the moment that mercy triumphed over judgment.

The Bible declares that our sinful nature will not and cannot please God (Romans 8:5-8). There is no way we can earn forgiveness for our sins or earn His love. But, because of His mercy, He sent Jesus Christ. Mercy is His character-His compassion, love, and kindness towards us. And yes, so often in life, we struggle, and we have disappointments. And though life can hurt us deeply, please remember to find the mercy of God.

Ephesians 2:4-5 reads, *"But God, being rich in mercy, because of His great love with which He loved us, even when we were dead in our transgressions, made us alive together with Christ (by grace you have been saved) ..."* "Being rich in mercy..." even when we were dead? That is the love of God. Because of His mercy, the Lord didn't just stop at salvation. 1 John 1: 9 states, "If you confess your sins, He will forgive you." Even as believers, He knows that we mess up. So, God made provisions to forgive us again and again. He is faithful to forgive you and will cleanse you from all unrighteousness. God is a wonderful Father.

If you do not have the benefit of a loving natural father and do not understand the power of a father's love... pray and ask God to show you, His love. There's nothing greater than having God as your Father, who speaks, guides, and leads us. (Proverbs 3:5) Question-are you grieving the heart of God because He keeps lavishing His love and mercy on you, but you have never fully received Him? Do you truly live in His mercy? Or are you still living like your Father God is not there?

One of the many reasons we are not able to receive or walk fully in His mercy and phenomenal love is because of our own pain. We are frustrated with life and angry with God. Even still, you can go to God and talk to Him about it. That is what lamentations mean, and it is called lamenting. You can tell God, "I'm hurt and disappointed." Will God heal you if you ask Him? Of course, He will heal your body and heart, too. He said, "I come to heal the brokenhearted" (Isaiah 61:1-3).

Some years ago, I asked God, "Why was I born in my family?" Of course, we don't choose our families. But God knew exactly what family He brought you through. It was all part of His design for you. He knew the DNA and genetic factors He needed. He knew the pressures on your personality and what circumstances you needed to call to Him. He knows all things. He created this family environment to equip you for His transformational purposes (Psalms 139).

But then again, transformation can take longer than it should because we keep resisting Him, right? Please go to God, take your pain, and tell Him, "Lord, I'm hurting, and I'm angry; please help me. I need Your healing touch. Tell Him about your struggles and fears. God responds to genuine confession because He wants truth in our innermost being (Psalm 51). He can work with truth because you finally recognize that you need Him.

The Holy Spirit is hindered when we try to fix ourselves. You cannot heal yourself or the people you love. You can pray for them. You can support them. You can even encourage them. But all of us must approach God according to His will to get what we need. Do not be afraid to approach Him because He is merciful and kind. (Hebrews 4:14-16). So, pray, "Dear Lord, I need You to help me to submit to Your will for my life." When are you going to believe Him and walk fully in His love and mercy? His word says, "I'm rich in mercy, and because of His great love towards you, He is patient."

God wants us to understand His mercy, which triumphed over judgment. He is not judging you at this time; He is loving you. Since God loves you and His mercy is new for you every morning, you can show mercy to others. This current life is our opportunity to reflect His love and mercy towards others. We must grasp the truth about mercy, understand His love for us, and receive it so that we can love ourselves and live fully as loved children of God.

His Presence

"If we know that we should seek God, we are debtors to our knowledge until we find Him." -Frangipane 1986[v]

The Bible declares that we live, move, and have our being in God. (Acts 17:28) And yet, so often, we feel so far away from Him-guilty about our sporadic prayer life and not always sure about how to improve it. Truthfully, most of us have times of spiritual highs and other times, we secretly wonder if God is really there. You might ask, is it really possible to sense the presence of God on a regular basis? Yes, it is possible and reasonable for any person who has received the gift of salvation by faith in Jesus Christ!

But first, we have to make time for God. Time is needed for solitude, silence, and the renewing of the mind. We need solitude and silence because we are so easily distracted by the cares of this life. Take time to rest in Him and wait quietly before Him. With earnest expectation, every believer should long to commune with God. Approaching God begins with the condition of our hearts. The Bible reveals that besides a faith that pleases God (Hebrews 11:6), a few other qualities of the heart are important. Truth about my heart in light of knowing God is essential.[v]

Only the Lord knows the truth about the condition of our hearts. A prayer asking the Lord to reveal our sins is necessary so that we can receive His forgiveness. The Lord is faithful in responding to this prayer because He also desires to commune with us. When God's light shines in our hearts, our next response is the awareness of how desperately we need the cleansing power of the Holy Spirit. Once our sins are revealed, we confess our sins to God and receive His forgiveness and cleansing. (1 John 1:9)

In addition, we know that God resists the proud but gives grace to the humble (James 4:6). This means that we need humility to draw near to God. Humility is the state of heart and mind that unites us with the need for His grace. As we worship Him with our lips, a wellspring of love for God overflows, and we sense the depth of His love and mercy toward us. This moves us to a time of seeking the Sovereign Lord with our whole hearts as we surrender all to Him. It is at that moment of total surrender that our hearts are prepared to commune with the Master!

There is nothing more wonderful than experiencing the manifest presence of God. Words are not adequate to describe His presence, but you sense love and life running like rivers of living water. God is so beautiful. You are awestruck and speechless. Actually, all you can do is weep tears of joy and love for God with gratitude while lingering quietly in His marvelous presence. Your soul is quieted and restful in His presence. Yes, we can experience His presence as often as we are willing to draw near as we worship and adore Him. God desires intimate communion with us. Jesus died to have a relationship with us.

The Spirit of God dwells in us and jealously desires an audience with our soul. James 4:5

His Rest

"So there remains a Sabbath rest for the people of God." (Hebrews 4:9)

There is still a place in God where believers can rest in Him and find peace for their souls. God used Himself to demonstrate the importance of rest. He created the heavens and everything on the earth in six days, and on the seventh day, He rested (Genesis 2:1-3). Observing the Sabbath was included in the Ten Commandments when established in the wilderness for the people of God (Exodus 20:8). In the Old Testament, the purpose of the Sabbath was to rest from your labor, for repentance, atonement and to humble your soul before the Lord (Leviticus 16:30-32).

God admonished in Isaiah that no one can build an earthly house for Him to dwell or rest. But He would dwell with the humble, repentant person who has an awesome reverence for His Word.

"Thus says the LORD, "Heaven is My throne and the earth is My footstool. Where then is a house, you could build for Me? And where is a place that I may rest? "For My hand made all these things, thus all these things came into being," declares the LORD. "But to this one I will look, to him who is humble and contrite of spirit, and who trembles at My word" (Isaiah 66:1-2).

In the Gospels, Jesus encourages us to come to Him to find rest, and before His ascension, He left His peace for us (John

14:27). *Come to Me, all who are weary and heavy-laden, and I will give you rest. 29 Take My yoke upon you and learn from Me, for I am gentle and humble in heart, and YOU WILL FIND REST FOR YOUR SOULS. 30 For My yoke is easy and My burden is light (Matthew 11:28-30).*

God warns us in Hebrews Chapters 3 and 4 that God's people heard some good news in the wilderness (the good news has been preached to us), but it did not profit them because they did not believe. That unbelief resulted in disobedience.

Although God's Sabbath rest was established during Creation, only His people can access His rest. Then again, in the wilderness, God was angered because the people would not believe His promises. So, they did not enter His rest. All of the unbelieving people died in the wilderness. Only two people from the original group entered the Promised Land, Caleb, and Joshua. God let Moses see the Promised Land, but he could not enter with the people. The warning in this passage says that when you hear His voice, do not harden your heart. It goes on to say, make sure you don't have an evil, unbelieving heart that is falling away from the living God...and be sure to encourage each other so that your heart is not hardened by the deceitfulness of sin. (Hebrews 3:12-18)

For many years, I thought that rest meant– work, work, serve, and work some more, and when exhausted, go find a quiet place to sleep or take a vacation. But I never really rested on vacation because I was too busy vacationing. Actually, I never learned how to rest because all I knew how to do was work. Even when I watched television, I would have my laptop on and working. In other words, I was always "on" and never unplugged. I only turned it off as I fell into bed and sleeping by the time my head hit the pillow.

As I learned more about spiritual disciplines and intimacy, I thought that rest was quiet time with worship music, devotionals, or specific prayer times. Although these disciplines are most beneficial to our spiritual health, His rest is far more than moments of intentional worship. When Jesus said, come and learn of me, He wanted to teach us a deeper truth about rest. Jesus lived in a constant state of rest. His rest was not episodic or impacted by external circumstances. He said come closer, spend time with Me, and let Me teach you how to be gentle and humble in heart, for this is where you will find rest.

When you decide to humble yourself and yield, He will come and rest with you. Humility is a condition of the heart that God responds to with His grace. Humility is when you are corrected or reproved by His Word, and you confess your sins so that the light of His presence can rest in your soul. It is when you sense His prompting and not ignore it or harden your heart.

A humble and gentle heart knows that whenever God speaks, we must honor His voice, listen, and agree. We should never take His Voice or Word for granted or treat it as common or like obedience is optional. The Lord cannot rest in an unbelieving heart, a disobedient heart, or a heart with unconfessed sin. His rest comes when we are willing to trust Him without hesitation, casting our cares upon Him-when we are humble before Him, willing to hear Him.

The scripture goes on to say that the blood of Jesus gives us the power to stop the endless activities of dead works and the freedom to serve the living God (Hebrews 9:14). Sabbath rest is the Promised Land of His abiding presence. His rest is most certainly present when we submit to the living God, resist evil, and draw near to Him (James 4:7-9). The Sabbath rest that remains is His enduring presence in a heart that is humbled, open, and awed by Him.

His Word

"For the word of God is alive and powerful..." (Hebrews 4:12a,)

God is present in His written Word, The Holy Bible. His Spirit illuminates His written Word and reveals the message of life to us. The Holy Bible is the written Word, and Jesus is the Word, and the Word is God. (John 1) *"The Word gave life to everything that was created, and his life brought light to everyone."* And God the Father breathed into chosen scribes to put His Words to paper (2 Peter 1:19-21).

When you search the scriptures, you will find Jesus. *"You search the Scriptures because you think that in them you have eternal life; it is these that testify about Me; and you are unwilling to come to Me so that you may have life...For if you believed Moses, you would believe Me, for he wrote about Me. But if you do not believe His writings, how will you believe My words?" (John 5:39, 40, 46 and 47)*

His presence is powerful, and because God is present in His Word, He can speak the Words of life and discern the Intentions of our hearts. *"For the Word of God is living and powerful, and sharper than any two-edged sword, piercing even to the division of soul and spirit, and of joints and marrow, and is a discerner of the thoughts and intents of the heart. And there is no creature hidden from His sight, but all things are naked and open to the eyes of Him to whom we must give account." (Hebrews 4:12-13)*

The Holy Bible clearly states its purposes for us. "...which are able to give you the wisdom that leads to salvation through faith which is in Christ Jesus. *"All Scripture is **inspired** by God and is useful to teach us what is true and to make us realize what is wrong in our lives. It corrects us when we are wrong and teaches us to do what is right."* (2 Timothy 3:15-17)

The Word of God lives forever. *"Heaven and earth will pass away, but My words will not pass away."* (Matthew 24:35)

WALKING WITH GOD

God Has a Plan

Today, our scripture readings reminded me that God chose us --We did not choose God. (John 15:16) He also called many of us to serve him as parents, church workers, educators, employees, and sacred ministry. And although we struggle through many life challenges, it does not alter our assignment from God. Many of our biblical characters endured numerous difficulties as they served God.

- King David was afraid and fought many battles. He was destitute and ran from King Saul for 14 years before he was crowned King.
- Joseph was beaten, thrown in a ditch for dead, sold into slavery, lied on and put in prison. From the time he was a teenager until he was 30 years old, he suffered numerous afflictions.
- Apostle Paul was beaten many times, ran for his life, and was dishonored, and he was hungry, imprisoned, and made to look like a fool while doing hard labor to support his ministry work.

Even Jesus Christ suffered many distresses while he ministered. Scriptures speak about his sadness, weeping, physical weariness, and grief. He even avoided crowds that only sought him for what he could do for them. Let us not forget the ultimate assignment: he paid the sin penalty by death on the cross for all of us!

I am encouraged by these stories because all chosen ones had confidence that God was with them. They also knew that difficulties in life did not mean that God was not watching over them to provide for and protect them. Nor did difficulties cancel their assignment from God. God used those trials to prepare them for His assignment.

As someone who has accepted His call to ministry, these scriptures help me to reaffirm my commitment to keep my vow to God. I am encouraged to remember that God is always with me. And when I'm afraid or feel attacked, I can trust His protection and security. And when life gets hard, I can lean on God to hide me under his wings. And when I am tempted to protect my honor, I remember that turning the other cheek, loving my enemies, and sacrificing for the good of others is God's way. And I don't have to depend on my wisdom; I can live by His principles. When we live according to God's principles, we live by the power of God. (1 Cor 4:20)

Psalm 56: 3-4, 8-13
3 But when I am afraid,
   I will put my trust in you.
4 I praise God for what he has promised.
   I trust in God, so why should I be afraid?
   What can mere mortals do to me?
8 You keep track of all my sorrows.
   You have collected all my tears in your bottle.
   You have recorded each one in your book.
9 My enemies will retreat when I call to you for help.
   This I know: God is on my side!
10 I praise God for what he has promised;
   yes, I praise the LORD for what he has promised.

11 I trust in God, so why should I be afraid?
   What can mere mortals do to me?
12 I will fulfill my vows to you, O God,
   and will offer a sacrifice of thanks for your help.
13 For you have rescued me from death;
   you have kept my feet from slipping.
  So now I can walk in your presence, O God,
   in your life-giving light.

Worship the Lord

I will bless the LORD at all times; His praise shall continually be in my mouth. My soul will make its boast in the LORD; The humble will hear it and rejoice. O magnify the LORD with me, and let us exalt His name together. Psalms 34: 1-3

When we think about worship, we should consider His Holy Spirit, Truth, and Presence. We need to know God and know ourselves in the light of God.[vi] The truth about God, self and our relationship with God is essential to biblical worship.

His Worshipers
*But the hour is coming, **and** now is when the true worshipers will worship the Father **in spirit and truth**, for the Father is seeking such to worship Him. God is **Spirit, and** those who worship Him must worship **in spirit and truth**."*[vii]

"And you shall know the truth, and the truth shall make you free."[viii]

Worship in the holy scriptures is defined as (toward)-kuneo (to kiss) signifies "to come forward and kiss." To kiss is to make intimate contact with another person. Similarly, we make contact with God in the most personal, intimate way when we touch Him as the divine Spirit in our human spirit.[ix]

Worship is a matter of the heart and an expression of our inner relationship with God; it may also be a public expression of a corporate relationship with Jesus. Worship is a lifestyle.

Therefore, I urge you, brethren, by the mercies of God, to present your bodies a living and holy sacrifice acceptable to God, which is your spiritual service of worship. ˣ

Delight yourself in the Lord; And He will give you the desires of your heart. Psalms 37:4

Yield now and be at peace with Him; Thereby good will come to you. Please receive instruction from His mouth, and establish His words in your heart. Job 22: 21-22 (23-30)

What happens when we worship God?
- We hallow (sanctify) His name
- We magnify and call Him Holy
- We focus on His wonderfulness

We do not ask God for what we want or need when we worship the Lord. We only seek His presence and not His provisions. We make God the center of our adoration because the Lord God is what we need; nothing and no one else is like our God. Hallelujah!

We should also think correctly about His sovereignty and our yielded heart towards Him. When you experience the manifest presence of our holy God, you realize how unworthy you are and how much you need His forgiveness. You also feel so grateful that God would allow you to be in His presence. As you are caught up in the beauty of His presence, you recognize that all is well.

What does God love to see when we worship Him?
He wants to see His Holy Spirit in our hearts and...
- **Pure heart** - God blesses those whose hearts are pure, for they will see God.[xi]

- **Surrendered/repented heart** - *Therefore, repent and return so that your sins may be wiped away so that times of refreshing may come from the presence of the Lord.*[xii]

- **Humble/contrite spirit** - *"But to this one, I will look, to him who is humble and contrite of spirit, and who trembles at My word*[xiii]

- **Circumcised heart** - *And the* LORD *your God will circumcise your heart and the heart of your descendants, to love the* LORD *your God with all your heart and soul so that you may live.*[xiv]

Why do we worship God?
- Because He is God: He is the great I AM!
- Only God deserves worship and adoration.
- It is the will of God and **a privilege only for believers**
- To sense His presence and worship him some more
- To bless God and be a place where God can rest

Question - Are you a resting place for God?
Thus says the LORD,
"Heaven is My throne, and the earth is My footstool.
Where then is a house you could build for Me?
And where is a place that I may rest?
2 "For My hand made all these things, Thus, all these things

came into being," declares the LORD.
"But to this one, I will look, to him who is humble
and contrite of spirit and trembles at My word.[xv]

Let us pray
Lord, we worship and adore You and bow down before You. Hallowed by thy Name in all the heavens and the earth. Our great honor and privilege are to magnify and sanctify you in our hearts! We are awed by You and so blessed to be in Your presence. Holy are You, Lord God Almighty! Amen

For we who worship by the Spirit of God are the ones who are truly circumcised. We rely on what Christ Jesus has done for us. We put no confidence in human effort.[xvi]

Our Provider

Jesus feeds the five thousand. John 6:1-15

The first thing that strikes me about this story of Jesus feeding more than 5000 people is that he planned the feeding and used available food and his disciples to make it happen. Even though Jesus knew the crowd was following him to see miraculous healings, he gave them what they needed. Jesus could have rained down manna from heaven, but he used what was available to him: a child's lunch.

God cares about our basic needs like food, clothes, and shelter. Too often, we focus on what we want and are unaware of what we need. But our Lord knows and works through our natural lives to provide spiritual and practical needs for daily living. And knowing that our God is working to give us what we need makes me feel so loved and protected. I believe that God gives all of us the ability to help others. As a servant, I feel so honored to be one of the many tools God uses to provide for His people. You may not have the time to serve at a food distribution center. But you could donate money, collect food, or lend your gifts and talents to encourage others to help people in need.

As we share the love of Christ, be sure to use his examples to meet needs. Please know that it is difficult for people to think about spiritual matters when they are hungry, sick, burdened with bills, and not having enough to provide for their loved ones. God cares about the whole person, and we should care about that, too.

These bible verses in 1 John 3:17-18 say it best...
*"But whoever has the world's goods, and sees his brother in need and closes his heart against him, how does the love of God abide in him? **18** Little children, let us not love with word or with tongue, but in deed and truth." (NASB)*

Grace Apprehended

The Bible has a lot to say about grace. We sing about grace, and it is impossible to talk about the goodness of God without the mention of grace. Likewise, most of the Book of Romans discusses this wonderful concept of grace. I also noticed that the words grace and gift are used interchangeably in the Bible. They have the same root word, Charis (a gift of grace)– we get our word charisma. Roman 6:23: "For the wages of sin is death, but the gift of God is eternal life in Christ Jesus our Lord. The point is that grace is a gift that comes from God.

"For by grace you have been saved, through faith" Eph. 2:8
"My grace is sufficient for you" 2 Cor. 12:9
"And God is able to make all grace abound to you" 2 Cor. 9:8
"We can go to the "throne of grace" Heb 4:16
"We are "justified by grace" Titus 3:7

Grace: The biblical concept of grace is much greater than what is suggested in the common understanding of "unmerited favor." It is not just the typical understanding that God shows us favor when He sent His Son, Jesus, to save us from our sins. A clearer understanding of biblical grace will radically change how you see life and your relationship with God. [xvii] Grace suggests that:

1. **The attitude of God towards us is one of acceptance and love.**
    You did not earn grace, and there was nothing you did to deserve it. You did not get it because you were good, cute,

intelligent, abused, or downtrodden. It is not about who you are or even what you have done. It is about the heart of God. He accepts us and loves us without hesitation! This is His fundamental disposition towards us; we are accepted and loved. *"God so loved the world that He gave..." John. 3:16*

2. **Grace is a dramatic statement about the human condition. Grace says that we are helpless, trapped in sin and incapable of pleasing God or winning His favor.** Religion, good works, and the law cannot fix us, save us, or make us better. The only way we can please God is to reject our reliance on self, the law, religion and rely completely on God. *We were dead in our sins; "we all have sinned and come short, our righteousness is as filthy rags..." Romans 3:25*

3. **Grace is a statement of a wonderful victory that God in Christ has acted, and He has come to the aid of all who will trust Him for their eternal salvation.** We need to know that we can confidently approach the throne of God when we need mercy for our sins and grace to help in a time of need. Heb 4: 16, Titus 2: 4-7 Grace is a way of life. Relying totally on Jesus to work within us, we experience God's unlimited power, vitalizing us and enabling us to live truly good lives. It is not what we do or how hard we try; we cannot improve ourselves. *"For in him we live, move and have our being..." Acts 17:28*

4. **Only the power and the presence of God can produce righteousness.** If we truly understood the nature of grace,

we would completely reject any confidence in ourselves and trust totally in Jesus, who alone cannot only declare us righteous men and women of God but also make us so! We can only live by a full commitment to the way of grace and all that grace involves. When we trust in the law or religion, we do not trust in God. When we try to earn favor from God by being good or doing the right thing in our strength, we are not living by the understanding that only God can help us to live right, talk right and have the right intentions or motives.

Apprehend means to grasp with understanding, recognize the meaning and arrest or seize. It is a wonderful word. We do not use this word very often, but it is powerful! So, knowing this word or knowing about grace is not enough; we have to do what apprehend means: arrest, seize and grab hold of grace.

The Lord not only gives you grace and mercy when you need it. Grace is always available to you, and grace is sufficient for all of life. When you are weak, God is strong![xviii] We have to believe in God by faith, and we must grab hold of His grace. Having confidence that grace is there for you. We must accept, walk in, and allow grace to shape our thinking, behavior, disposition, and attitude.

When you understand that God is gracious to you, it will help you to be gracious towards yourself and others. Also, we will become more forgiving, loving, and able to show mercy to ourselves and others. Because now you understand how pitiful you are and how you do not deserve mercy from a holy, sinless, and perfect God, yet His mercy is new every morning.

Please understand that it is not that you are going to get grace. His grace has always been there. He has always been gracious. We ask and pray for grace, but we already have grace from God. We need to walk in that understanding. We acknowledge our weaknesses and acknowledge that God has given us the grace to handle all situations. Confronting any difficult issue can be hard, but His grace is with you! If a difficult season is upon you right now, so is His grace.

We must know with confidence that we have the grace of God. The confidence is not in people or self but in who God says He is; his very essence is grace. The moment I acknowledge that I am weak and need God, I become strong. His power is made perfect in my weaknesses. We should brag about being weak, not for the sake of weakness, but for the sake of needing God. 2 Cor. 12:9-10

I can tell when I am not walking in His grace. Because I worry, I get scared, and I try to fix problems with my strength. Yes, we can get frustrated with our situations and complain about the devil while still trying to do self-repairs. So often, we trust in the works of our hands and idolize people and things. And still wonder why we have no victory as believers. It is because we have not seized grace by faith (apprehended) to allow it to change our worldview.

This truth is so important to our relationship with God. If you want to experience the benefits of His grace, please ask the Lord to give you a divine understanding in your heart. It will transform the way you understand God and your relationship with Him.

I want all that God has for me. I want to live by grace, understand, grasp, seize, and walk therein! I want to automatically cast my cares upon Jesus because He cares for me. I want to make sure I fully rely on His grace, which is His acceptance and love!

Finally, I pray that all of us will rely on His grace together. Amen

The River of Giving

God loves a cheerful giver.[xix] When we begin to give cheerfully with confidence in the Lord, it proves that God is doing supernatural work in us. The river of giving is how His blessings flow to us in response to our obedience to give. [xx] First, the Lord is working his faith in us to believe His promises of abundance that flow through our giving. Secondly, He is doing spiritual work by expanding our hearts to care for others. Giving is a spiritual principle established by God. His river of giving includes more than just material resources because spiritual blessings and protection are part of the flow. So, let us not limit our understanding of His spiritual work in the river of giving.

Once God can trust us with giving or be sensitive to his leading when He wants us to give, we will experience an abundance beyond natural resources. Our sense of connectedness to God increases, our capacity to care for others expands, and we walk with a gracious, confident joy from the Lord. These are just a few of the priceless blessings flowing in the river of giving. The spiritual principle of overflow (increase) means that the Lord will always ensure we have more than enough to share with others. It also means that the more you sow (give), the more you reap (receive) in the harvest. So, the more we trust God to give, the more God can trust us with more resources, spiritual graces, and blessings.

There is a spiritual river of giving that flows from God through us to others. Many think the biblical principle of "if you, then I will" is reciprocal or equal, but it is not. We can never compare our limited capacity to obey God to his supernatural response. The Lord God is always free to do new and surprising things for us. His loving intention and plans for us are beyond what we could imagine.[xxi]

Material resources and gifts pale in comparison to His love, favor, presence, healing, and wholeness as we grow in Him.

A Journey with Fears and Faith

"The LORD is my light and my salvation; whom shall I fear? The LORD is the strength of my life; of whom shall I be afraid?" (Psalm 27:1 NKJV)

I was reading Psalm 27 today...and I confess that these words are incongruent with my current heart condition. I am afraid, and yes, I do have fears. I sensed the Spirit of the Lord asking me and answering at the same time. He told me that I was afraid of Him. Afraid of what He might allow and afraid of what the future may hold for my son and his family. I have so much fear related to my son's health. I'm afraid that he will not take care of himself, that some sudden illness or current illness will overtake him and kill him. I am so tormented by the fear of losing him. And I am disappointed because I have already felt the loss of the healthy him, the funny him, the creative singing him. All of the many complications and surgeries have left me and all of us traumatized, frustrated, sad, and angry. I'm so upset because my son has been so sick over these last few years.

Yes, the Word of God declares that perfect love casts out fear... I recognized the torment that comes from fear, but this fear is not about my life or future, and I have such confidence and faith in God's love, mercy, and grace for me. I know, without hesitation, that God loves me. He means me well; I'm confident I will be in heaven with Him. But I am so hurt about my son's illness and how it has impacted all of us. My faith (confidence and trust) is very low, and God's love is not perfected in me regarding how I feel about my son. I have not totally cast my cares about my son on the Lord. And yes, I'm having a tantrum because of so much perceived loss.

I went from fear to anger, lack of faith, and imperfect love. Clearly, there are several connecting parts that need to be unraveled. I know that I have grace for my trials, but I need grace for my family's trials as well. I must start trusting God to help me deal with these fears. First, I need to make peace with the past (healing, forgiveness, and acceptance). Secondly, I need to ask for grace to agree with God's sovereignty and give my cares to Him. Finally, I need to learn more about Jesus and take on His yoke (easy, with light burdens). I must believe that His Intentions are only good for my family, just like they are for me.

Lord, here I am again, looking to You for your grace, faith, and love. Thank You for helping me find peace in You.

Update: It has been ten years since I wrote this message. My son is still with us! The Lord reminded me during this time that I cannot love my son more than He can. Again, we must align our will for our families with God's will for them. We want our children to have a wonderful, problem-free life. But all of us have struggles and trials in life. We also want them to have a good life, but God wants them to have eternal life! As soon as I began to shift my focus towards trusting God with my family and reassuring myself that God loves them best and that His goal is heaven, the worry and fear melted away. And every time those thoughts try to return, I reject them and remember that God loves them best! My prayers for them have shifted from fretful begging to a confident acknowledgment that God is taking care of them. Today, my son is a wonderful father and husband. He manages his health so much better. And still, his great sense of humor continues to bless us as he continues to sing on occasion. But most importantly, his walk with God and the salvation of his family continues to be a reality. The Lord is a wonderful and faithful heavenly Father. Praise the Lord!

A Scene from Heaven!

"You are worthy, O Lord, to receive glory and honor and power; for You created all things, and by Your will they exist and were created." (Revelation 4:11, NKJV)

When we look at this scene in heaven, we see every living creature bowing before the King, crying, "Holy, Holy, Holy!" Wow! How appropriate that the Lord God receives honor, all glory, and all praise because, after all, He created us because He wanted to, right? These things are too awesome for me! His holiness is beyond my ability to fully comprehend. But, when I think about Him who sits on the throne, my only response is to worship Him! What else is there to do when you stand in His presence? We are His creation, His redemptive work, and the objects of His great love. He chose to create us, redeem us, and prepare us for heaven so that we can be with Him forever; what great love! No other created being other than mankind can declare that they have been redeemed by the Holy One.

I was lost in sin with a desperately wicked heart-with nothing to offer God but brokenness and despair. But God sent His Son, Jesus Christ, to pay the price for my pitiful soul. And not only did He purchase me with His own blood (Acts 28:20), He also sent His Holy Spirit to live in my heart to transform me into His likeness-because He wants me to look like Him! My, my, my... I worship You today, Lord!

SPIRITUAL FRUIT

Sweet Fruit

"But the fruit of the Spirit is love, joy, peace, patience, kindness, goodness, faithfulness, gentleness, self-control; against such things there is no law." (Galatians 5:22)

While doing some research on natural fruit trees, I learned that it takes dedication, time, and patience to grow sweet fruit. Here are some things to consider when growing sweet fruit: the quality of the seed, the soil, water, temperature, and agents to protect the tree from attack. There is a certain time to prepare the ground, plant, water, prune, and feed. A crucial step we must not neglect is to prepare the ground for the seed. You must plant in the right season because it is the optimal time for the seed to germinate and grow. Weather is unpredictable, so you must have a plan to create the right climate. It takes several years before trees are ready to produce sweet fruit. Although fruit grows in the first year or two, it is too small and bitter. In these first few years, trained growers will aid healthy growth by cutting off immature fruit.

This research caused me to think about the spiritual implications of the fruit of the Spirit, such as how we need to better understand the principles of sweet spiritual fruit and how we can use similar principles to improve our relationship with the Holy Spirit. What is spiritual fruit? Well, in general, fruit is the end product of a growth process or the relationship between branches and trees. In a spiritual context, you cannot have spiritual fruit without having a relationship with the Holy Spirit.

If you are a Christian, saved by the gracious work of Jesus Christ, the Spirit of God has made a connection with you. In other words, when you become a Christian, you have the necessary connection for Jesus to produce His fruit. The Bible says that Jesus is the vine (tree), we are the branches, and God is the Gardener (John 15).

You have to be connected to Jesus to bear spiritual fruit. And God takes care of the vine and its branches. In short, the quality of your relationship with Jesus impacts the quality of your spiritual fruit.

Therefore, we must consider this question, "How sweet is my fruit?" Is your spiritual fruit small and bitter to the taste? Are you still a spiritual baby, not able to digest the meat of His love through the Word of God? Has your tree been developing for a while but still not producing the fruit of the Spirit, indicated by His life-giving love, freedom not to sin, mercy, and joy? Are you still a bench warmer and not a disciple or teacher? Are you still carrying bitterness from your past or having tantrums when things do not go your way? Are you blaming God for your trials, and you are not willing to forgive disappointments and let go of the cares of this world? Do you still struggle with loving your enemies? If you answered yes to any of these questions, I suggest that you check for connection problems in your growth process with the Lord.

Let us review the spiritual growth process: Was the right seed planted; Jesus Christ is the Word? What kind of soil (heart condition) was the Word planted in-shallow, rocky, or good ground? How nutritious is your spiritual diet? Do you have a regular diet of the Word of God? Do you have fellowship with believers, singing and praying with thanksgiving? Are the rivers of living water flowing through your life by sharing your faith, making disciples, and offering practical service? Are you in an environment that promotes spiritual growth, a church that worships God, cares about and nurtures your life in Christ, and teaches its members to reach the lost? Have you given yourself time to grow in the Lord? Has your fruit been pruned, faith tested in adversity, with sprouts of patience growing? Do you have pesticides for the "little foxes that spoil the vines" and the sin that so easily ensnares you (Hebrews 12:1-3, Song of Solomon 2:15)? Do you practice the instructions in the Book of James 4:7-8 that says, Submit to God, resist the devil and he will flee from you. Draw near to God and He will draw near to you…"?

Most people love sweet fruit. Honestly, my family prefers junk food over nutritional snacks, but when I offer sweet fruit, it goes faster than the junk food. Spiritual fruit is like natural fruit. The sweeter the fruit, the quicker people are willing to consume it. But, if it is small, bruised, and bitter, you cannot pay a person to eat it. Our Lord called us to share our faith with the world and to help believers grow in love (Ephesians 4:16). How can we share the Light of God if our fruit is bitter and nobody wants it? Please fix your connections with the Lord by having a submitted heart, a vibrant prayer life, spending time in God's Word, and fellowship with fruit-bearing believers. Please make sure His life-giving Spirit is free to flow through you. We need sweet-tasting spiritual fruit so that we can reflect the love of God on the earth and multiply the crop (reach the lost) to glorify our heavenly Father. Amen!

John 15:5-8

5 "Yes, I am the vine; you are the branches. Those who remain in me, and I in them, will produce much fruit. For apart from me you can do nothing. 6 Anyone who does not remain in me is thrown away like a useless branch and withers. Such branches are gathered into a pile to be burned. 7 But if you remain in me and my words remain in you, you may ask for anything you want, and it will be granted! 8 When you produce much fruit, you are my true disciples. This brings great glory to my Father.

Anger, Healing, and Forgiveness

One day, I asked the Lord, "Why am I so sad?" Amazingly, the Lord revealed that it was not sadness but anger. He said to me, "Your anger feels like sadness because you have pushed it down and tried to smother it. Your anger has been suppressed, and you feel depressed because your anger has been turned inward. Your anger is simmering like a slow boil. When it bubbles up, or you silence yourself long enough to feel the simmer, you think it is sadness. Your anger has affected your energy, slowed you down, and stifled your joy."

Yes, Lord, I prayed, "I am a victim of my anger. I am in prison and going through the motions and duties of life. I have not been able to enjoy life, love goodness, or Your grace." I am frustrated because I feel like I am being ungrateful towards God and disappointed because I have not been enjoying the many blessings from Him. I cried out to Him, "Lord, I really need to know how to deal with anger." In the subsequent weeks, I did some research on anger. During my research, I realized that my anger is deeper than just the typical garden variety anger. The Lord revealed that I had a bitter root of anger. The Word of God teaches us not to fall short of the grace of God and let a bitter root spring up. (Hebrews 12:15) So, I prayed, "Lord, I need Your grace for healing and forgiveness. Help me, Lord. This root is deep, long, and old and may even be inherited. So, I pray and ask You, God, to wash me and cleanse me of any sins and ungodly beliefs. Please reveal areas of unconfessed sin and hurt and help me to walk correctly before You. Amen!"

Three sources of anger were revealed. I was hurt deeply at age 5, I was fearful, and my faith was challenged due to the illness of my son, and finally, there were some ancestral wounds from racism. So, I confessed and acknowledged the many sins that resulted from past violations, fears, and the bitter root. I continued to pray, "Lord, I only want to be guided by Your Spirit and truth. So again, Lord, I ask You to forgive me for living with unconfessed sins. I confess my sins and ask that You cleanse me from all unrighteousness. I have since learned to confess the sin of allowing the work of evil to operate in my life.

Heal me and help me to forgive those who have hurt me. Forgive me for wrongly blaming You and being angry with You for the evil that hurt me. Lord, I submit to You, so help me to walk by the power of Your presence and love. Lord, let me sense that I have completely surrendered to You and that I am not holding anything back. Thank You, Lord, for loving me, for walking with me, and for my life with You. Lord, I recognize that I must continue to surrender my will to You and resist the enemy's snares. I commit my life afresh to You. I need Your joy and peace as I live to reflect Your glory and love. My heart is broken before You, thank You, Lord."

During this same season, I was told that I had hurt someone many times with my sharp words and retaliatory posture. In addition, the person told me that they had not forgiven me as we spoke. I did not realize that I had hurt someone so deeply, to the point that they had shut down towards me. I apologized to them and asked if they would truly seek the Lord to help them forgive me. I prayed, "Lord, I asked that You forgive me for hurting them. I acknowledge my sins towards You and them. Please cleanse my heart and teach me Your ways. Lord, help me to forgive the person I hurt as well. Many times, I lashed out at them because of my feelings of isolation and emotional distance. Lord, forgive me for being like the people who hurt me!"

The Lord responded to my heart through His Word, "Behold, you desire truth in the innermost being, and in the hidden part You will make me know wisdom." (Psalms 51:6). I continued to pray, "Lord, flood me with the light of Your truth and wisdom. Help me to have internal integrity and transparency. Help my friend to heal and forgive again. Lord, I pray for both of us, and please forgive, heal, and teach us to walk humbly before You. Help me, Lord, to cast my cares upon You, and teach me to love those who hurt me and not retaliate. Help me to pray for those who hurt me. Help me to see and love them through Your grace. Thank You, Lord."

Today, I would also ask the Lord to bind the work of the enemy and help us to resist evil in our lives. I have so much to be thankful for, but I also know that I have to let myself experience anger and stop pushing it down. Actually, during this time, I was feeling a lot of anger. But it was too much anger for the issues at hand. I had been so angry that I was wrestling with how I should feel versus how I really felt. So, I decided not to approach anyone until after praying and waiting for His gracious leading. I have learned that anger is a surface feeling for deeper hurts.

I was still hurt about my parents not being there for me on so many levels. I had not completely forgiven them at that time. Now, certain things happen that trigger these feelings of hurt and abandonment and memories of being alone and scared. I am still prayerful and looking to the Lord. I asked the Lord to please help me to completely forgive my mother and my absent father. Thank God for the book, Chosen Vessels,[xxii] because it really helped me work through some painful areas that were hindering me from responding and being sensitive to God's leading. I am fully confident that God heard my prayers and will respond according to His love and best intentions for my life.

"Thank You, Lord, for helping me by revealing the need for more healing and wholeness. I need Your help to serve You with my whole heart, and I trust that You will address these areas in my life that prevent me from having a singleness of heart towards You." I recently attended a workshop called "Matters of the Heart." I was reminded of the various types of heart conditions, such as broken, attached, divided, hardened, contrite (remorseful), tender, and whole. So often, we are not faithful in our relationship with the Lord because of the condition of our hearts.

Only God can heal a broken and divided heart. Let us pray, "Lord, I am asking You to be greater than my heart, (1 John 3:20); bind up the brokenness and help me to be fully available to You. I forgive, forgive, and forgive. Lord, as always, I need Your help, mercy, and grace today and Your peace and joy, too. With much love and honor, Your child..."

During this time of revising some messages for this book, I have been amazed at the deep and marvelous work the Lord has performed in my life these past ten years. I decided to keep this message in this book because, we are human and I know that so many of us deal with the matters of a hurting heart. But I just want to share with you that now I sense these older writings were prophetic because the Lord has answered every prayer shared in these earlier writings! Of course, I am not complete yet, but I can see the spiritual growth in my life and the answers to the previous prayers of the past.

I am overwhelmed by His love and faithfulness. So, I can confirm that God's promises are true! The Lord blesses beyond what we could ever ask or think.[xxiii] And that eyes have not seen, and ears have not heard what God has in store for those who love Him.[xxiv] Although my journey is not over yet, I have been honored with the experience of seeing God move in my life to heal and set me free to declare His truth with confident conviction as living proof!

This book revision journey has been cathartic (liberating) for me. The blessings continue, and I am deeply grateful.

Bitterness and Grace

"Look after each other so that none of you fails to receive the grace of God. Watch out that no poisonous root of bitterness grows up to trouble you, corrupting many." (Hebrews 12:15, NLT)

The Lord admonishes us to look after each other and to make sure our hearts are clear before Him. This means that we make sure our hearts are free from offense, and we encourage others to forgive as well. Why? Because most human interaction gives the opportunity for us to take offense or to offend someone else. Bitterness comes from withholding forgiveness over a period of time. If we refuse to ask the Lord for help to forgive, an offense will grab hold of our hearts and take root. As it grows, it begins to poison how we feel, what we think, and how we relate to God and others. The root grows, and bitterness springs up.

This toxic root soon blooms and spills over to hurt others, which starts a new cycle of unforgiveness. It requires diligent effort and honesty to dislodge a bitter root in your heart. To overcome bitterness and forgive from our heart-we must spend time in prayer, have a willingness to forgive, confess it, and ask for supernatural healing and the power to let go of the pain associated with hurtful acts. Have you ever experienced a sense of heaviness that, no matter how hard you try, you cannot seem to shake it off? You try to increase your prayer life, church attendance, and Bible reading, but to no avail! When all else fails, you seek God and ask Him to search your heart to find the source of the heaviness. And He reveals that an unforgiven offense is lurking in your heart.

Our first response must be to confess our sins, turn back to God, and let Him wipe away every sin. Then, according to the Word, "times of refreshing will come from the presence of the Lord" (Acts 3:19). I must confess that refusing to forgive or being in denial about harboring anger and resentment in my heart is a reflection of my own lack of closeness with the Lord. It also speaks to my refusal to acknowledge God's love for me.

When I am struggling to forgive someone, it is because I have forgotten how much I have been forgiven and ALL of the gracious love God has bestowed on me while I was still in my sin! Bitterness makes our hearts turn cold, and at the same time, it hinders His loving influence in our lives. Consequently, the warm love that comes from His presence cannot shine through and touch others. When we are not influenced by His love, we fall short of His grace. Be assured that grace is an extraordinary gift from God. Grace is His blessings and undeserved favor to have eternal life…and life more abundantly (John 10:10). It is because He loved us first that He shed His own blood and paid the penalty for our sins! "For by grace you have been saved…" (Ephesians 2:8). God never intended for us to carry hurt and the weight of offenses. So, God made provisions for us to confess our sins and receive His forgiveness.

Bitterness is particularly harmful to believers because our hearts become distant from the Lord, rendering us incapable of showing love from a pure heart. Ultimately, we fail to witness to the world that Jesus Christ is real! It is incredible how, although we did not deserve His forgiveness, God knew we would commit sins even after salvation, so He made provision to forgive us (1 John 1:9).

Unfortunately, many believers will not follow His example and make provisions to forgive others. God promised that His "grace is sufficient in weakness, for when we are weak, He is strong." (II Cor. 12:9). Let us make sure we receive forgiveness from God and ask God to help us forgive others so that we can walk in His sufficient grace in our lives. Please don't miss out on the grace of God!

Joy in Trials

Have you ever felt like you had great faith or that you trusted God and were willing to do whatever He had in store for you? Have you ever prayed and asked the Lord to make you a better Christian? Or told God that you loved Him and wanted to be all you could be for Him? But then, a very difficult trial happens, and now life becomes really hard. And you also notice that you are more frustrated and dissatisfied and have no joy. Your faith is not so robust, and you question God, right?

Next, the "why me Lord?" thoughts begin, not this, anything but this, Lord. Now, your faith is shaky, and you are thinking God made a mistake. Or He did not notice how the devil is still trying to kill and destroy you, right? To name a few of the most difficult trials in life. We ask, Lord, why did you allow my son to get so sick, or my daughter to get pregnant, my son to use drugs, my spouse to change for the worst, lose my job and my house, or get sick, lose a loved one, get sued for something you did not do and so forth.

Consider it all joy, my brethren, when you encounter various trials, 3 knowing that the testing of your faith produces endurance. 4 And let endurance have its perfect result, so that you may be perfect and complete, lacking in nothing. James 1:2

As I read the Word for help during my trial, I started in the Book of James. My first question was, why does the Word of

God say to have joy during difficult times? This phase stayed on my mind, "count it all joy." I thought the last thing people want to hear when they are going through is to count it all joy, right?

We also know that it takes patience and discernment when we help others. We are trained to listen to them with compassion, cry in sorrow and rejoice with them in victory or success. We empathize and express that we care about them before providing godly instructions.

So, before we discuss that word joy or even talk about the benefits of trials. We have to discuss fundamental truths about the Lord God to help us understand suffering in His Word. You will never understand suffering if you do not know who God is.

Two or three facts are needed as we come to know God through difficult times.

- o God is sovereign: all-powerful, everywhere present; knows everything and is intimately involved in our lives.

- o God is holy love: He is pure; there is no darkness or evil in God at all; not only does God love you, but He is love. The blood of Jesus Christ is the bridge and connection between us and Father God.

Difficulties in life will never make sense if we do not at least understand and believe these two facts about God. Oswald Chambers said it this way:

"Faith is not a pathetic sentiment, but robust, vigorous confidence built on the fact that God is holy love. You cannot see Him just now or understand what He is doing, but you know Him. Shipwreck occurs where there is no mental poise, which comes from being established on the eternal truth that God is holy love. Faith is the heroic effort of your life; you fling yourself in reckless confidence on God. God has ventured all in Jesus Christ to save us; now He wants us to venture out all in abandoned confidence in Him."[xxv]

Our relationship with God is not based on feelings or even circumstances but on faith (love) in God. When we trust that God loves us and cannot do evil toward us, he knows what He is doing and means you well. Then you can put difficult times in the proper context, which says, if God allows this, it must be for my good. This experience will help me, and it will work for my good. [xxvi]

Yes, we complain, and no, we do not like that trials are so hard, but we should never forget that God is holy love. We do not know God's full plan or our future, but we know God.

We know that God wants us to respond in faith, cast our cares on Him, and trust that even while God is working things out on our behalf, He is transforming us into the likeness of His son, Jesus Christ.

One of the reasons we can have joy when we encounter trials is that we know that God will use any trial as an opportunity to move us toward His hallmarks of growth in Him. Such as letting patience work in us so that one day, we can all declare, I lack nothing!

Count it all joy means having the right attitude during your trials. Because if we go through trials with vigorous and robust faith, knowing that only good can come out of this situation. And although we cannot see the good, we believe and trust God.

When your faith is tested, your patience should increase, and you will notice that you have more endurance. And if patience is completed, it will develop a maturity with wisdom and improved discernment.

16 Therefore, we do not lose heart, but though our outer man is decaying, our inner man is being renewed day by day. 17 For momentary, light affliction is producing for us an eternal weight of glory far beyond all comparison, 18 while we look not at the things which are seen, but at the things which are not seen; for the things which are seen are temporal, but the things which are not seen are eternal. 2 Cor 4:16-18

In summary, we will become mature believers who show forth the glory of God. God works out our troubles beyond what we could ever think or ask (remember that through every experience in life, God is working out His purpose for your life), and we get some rewards in heaven because we suffered hardship like a good soldier for God. Now, I think that is a pretty good deal, what about you?

¹² Blessed is a man who perseveres under trial; for once he has been approved, he will receive the crown of life which the Lord has promised to those who love Him. James 1:12

¹⁸ For I consider that the sufferings of this present time are not worthy to be compared with the glory that is to be revealed to us. Romans 8:18

So now, whenever you find yourself in a place where life is really hard, you already know that God is up to something truly good for you.

Yes, we all endure trials, but each time you walk through with faith in God and joy in your heart, you become more patient, and His grace is there to help ease your burden, as God uses our trials to build His character in us. This is evidenced by our growth in faith, joy, and wisdom when we face our next "light affliction." Hence, we all need to grab hold of God and hang on for the ride (blessing).

24 *Now to Him who is able to keep you from stumbling, and to make you stand in the presence of His glory blameless with great joy,* ***25*** *to the only God our Savior, through Jesus Christ our Lord, be glory, majesty, dominion, and authority, before all time and now and forever. Amen. Jude 24-25*

LIFE LESSONS

Remember the Basics

As the new year comes, the Lord reminds us not to forget our basic spiritual habits. Sometimes, we think we need a deep word or a special endowment when going through challenging times, but practicing these basic spiritual disciplines keeps us steady in the Lord.

- Remember to focus on the Word of God
- Remember to spend time with the Lord
- Remember to fellowship with other believers
- Remember to always pray

- **Keep the Word of God ever before you.**

The Word of God is food for the soul; truths that will set you free and heal the heart and mind. The word of God should be our focus, and we should read it daily. The scripture says…

> **Joshua 1:8**
> This Book of the Law shall not depart from your mouth, but you shall **meditate** in it day and night, which you may observe according to all written in it. For then you will make your way prosperous, and then you will have success.

> **John 8:31-32**
> 31 Jesus said to the people who believed in him, "You are truly my disciples if you remain faithful to my teachings. 32 And you will know the truth, and the truth will set you free."

Hebrews 4:12
For the word of God *is* living and powerful, and **sharper** than any two-edged sword, piercing even to the division of soul and spirit, and of joints and marrow, and is a discerner of the thoughts and intents of the heart.

- **Be sure to spend quiet time with the Lord**

Just rest in His presence and wait quietly before Him. Give the Lord some quality time daily. His presence is heaven to us!

Psalm 91:1
He who dwells in the **secret** place of the Most High shall abide under the shadow of the Almighty. I will say of the LORD, "*He is* my refuge and my fortress; My God, in Him I will trust."

Lamentations 3:22-26
22 *Through* the LORD's mercies we are not consumed, because His compassions fail not.
23 *They are* new every morning;
Great *is* Your faithfulness.
24 "The LORD *is* my portion," says my soul,
"Therefore I hope in Him!"
25 The LORD *is* good to those who wait for Him,
To the soul *who* seeks Him.
26 *It is* good that *one* should hope and wait quietly
For the salvation of the LORD.

Matthew 11:28-29

28 Come to Me, all *you* who labor and are heavy laden, and I will give you rest. **29** Take My yoke upon you and learn from Me, for I am gentle and lowly in heart, and you will find rest for your souls.

- **Fellowship with other Believers**

Fellowship with believers in your personal life, in worship service and with your work family alike. Be sure to spend time with other believers for strength, prayer, and encouragement. The Lord reminds us to encourage each other in fellowship to do what is right.

Hebrews 10:24-25

24 And let us consider one another in order to stir up love and good works, **25** not forsaking the assembling of ourselves together, as *is* the manner of some, but exhorting *one another,* and so much the more as you see the Day approaching.

Colossians 3:16-17

16 Let the word of Christ dwell in you richly in all wisdom, teaching and admonishing one another in psalms and hymns and spiritual songs, singing with grace in your hearts to the Lord. **17** And whatever you do in word or deed, *do* all in the name of the Lord Jesus, giving thanks to God the Father through Him.

1 John 1:7
But if we walk in the light as He is in the light, we have **fellowship** with one another, and the blood of Jesus Christ His Son cleanses us from all sin.

- **Remember to always pray**

Prayer is the life blood of our spiritual walk. Prayer keeps our mind on Jesus and helps us look to God for everything. The Bible says to always pray.

Philippians 4:6-7
6 Be anxious for nothing, but in everything by prayer and supplication, with thanksgiving, let your requests be made known to God; **7** and the peace of God, which surpasses all understanding, will guard your hearts and minds through Christ Jesus.

Ephesians 6:18
18 praying always with all prayer and supplication in the Spirit, being watchful to this end with all perseverance and supplication for all the saints

As we embark on another year, I encourage you to practice these lifestyle habits… and the Lord will keep you anchored in Him, no matter what life circumstances bring. Amen

Don't be Discouraged!

The Syrophoenician Woman

²⁸ Then Jesus told her, "O woman, your faith is great; it shall be done for you as you wish." And her daughter was healed at once. Matthew 15:28

God knows the heart of a mother…This praying woman had a lot going for her and we can learn a lot from her story. First, this story is about a mother with a sick child, a momma trying to get some help for her daughter… it was not the kind of help that a doctor, a counselor, or any other person could provide.

She did her research and found out who could help her. She knew that Jesus was the only one who could heal her child. No doubt she had been to everyone else… And she was tracking the whereabouts of Jesus and ready to ask when He came to her town. She knew how to approach the Lord and what to ask for:

- First, she asked for mercy.
- Then she worshipped Him and called him Lord.
- She acknowledged that He was the Messiah, the Son of David.
- She told Him what she needed.

She did not get an answer to her first request. **But that did not discourage her!** His disciples said, please say something or help her because she is not going away; she will not stop asking… **Even they knew she was desperate…**

So, Jesus said to her, my mission right now is to help the chosen people, the Jews, not Gentile dogs. Not only did He tell her no, he called her a negative name. **But that did not discourage her!** Because she knew that God is a great big God and can do abundantly, above all that we can ask or think. (Ephesians 3:20)

She agreed with Jesus and said, yes, I might be a dog, but you can bless me too! Because she knew that God rains on the just and the unjust… Her perspective was, call me whatever you want, but please bless me!

She probably felt that she did not deserve what the decent church folk deserved and was not trying to take what belonged to them; she just needed a few crumbs, just enough to help her baby. She knew that in God, there is enough mercy, grace, and blessings for all of us.

> *16 Therefore let us draw near with confidence to the throne of grace, so that we may receive mercy and find grace to help in time of need. Heb. 4:16*

Therefore, her confidence in God and her great faith in Jesus… stopped Him in His tracks… and He said, oh, I am going to bless you because your faith impressed Me. Her faith got His attention… and we know that without faith, we cannot please God.

Jesus had been looking all over Israel but had not found faith like this Gentile woman. Her great faith caused Jesus to answer her prayer. Jesus gave her what she needed, and her daughter was healed at that very moment. Praise God!

Don't give up on God because He is still looking for faith in the earth.

Rhythms of Grace

God wants to fill us up, make us plump like sweet grapes with the fruit of His presence (Holy Spirit). Not just to be sweet for the sake of being sweet. He wants to squeeze that river of living water out of our bellies to let His Spirit flow through us to reach His people. His desire is to transform us into the likeness of His son so that we can be light and salt.

God wants His word and message to come from Him, not us. That's why we have to spend time with Jesus, take up His yoke, and learn to live light and easy like Him. Not weary, heavy or burdened.[xxvii] But learn how to rest in Him and cast your cares upon him because He cares for us. How do we know that? Because we have been spending time with Him, and He has taught us the difference between what we should carry and what burdens belong to Him. The weapons of our warfare are not carnal. Many times, we are trying to fight spiritual enemies with natural weapons. [xxviii]

Unforced rhythms of grace are when you abide under the shadow of the Almighty and walk in His presence. You see things happening, good and bad. But the Lord teaches you how to wait on Him, rest in Him, commit to prayer and then watch God move.

When you finally agree with God that you can do nothing without Him.[xxix] God teaches you how to walk in that truth. The grace of God allows you to see your situation as improving, and you are aware that God is moving and not you. He is performing His will and plan in your life. Lord, we need you to help us stop trying to fix things we cannot.

You know that when we are weary and feel the burdens of life, we are carrying God's load! We try to fix situations because we get scared and do not trust God as we should. Dear Lord, help me to default on trusting you, especially during difficult times.

Some of you might think that I don't understand your situation. I may not, but God does, so spending time with Him will teach you that God understands all things and that nothing is too hard for Him.

Our rest, peace and joy come from believing that the Lord loves us and He only means us well. Even in difficult seasons, we must learn to go to God and trust Him with His loving plan. Go to the Lord in prayer and acknowledge that you don't know how to rest; ask Him to teach you. Be open and intentional about knowing God better. Look for Him in your heart, set aside quiet time, and find ways to learn of Him. Such as bible study, read a spiritual book or devotionals that encourage a relationship with the Lord, ask your Pastor, and search for God until you find Him.

God is not lost or missing, but we must give this most important teaching from the Lord our time and energy.

Forgiveness

"Do not let the hurts of your past hold your future captive."[xxx]

"But if you do not forgive others, then your Father will not forgive the wrongs you have done" (Matthew 6:15, GNT).

Does it seem like somebody is talking about forgiveness every time you turn around? You might think, "Why is forgiveness so important?" Let us look at a few scriptures in the Word of God:
- If you don't forgive from your heart, God will not forgive you. (Matthews 6:14-15)
- You cannot bring your gifts to God and pray, until you reconcile. (Matthews 5:23-25)
- A root of bitterness causes trouble and defiles many. (Hebrews 12:15)

What are these scriptures telling us? -Your prayers are hindered; you have an open account of unforgiveness with God, and your heart is bitter and defiling others. Well, maybe you keep hearing about forgiveness because God loves you and desires to make sure you are healed, set free from bitterness, and walk in the fullness of His love. So, answer this question, "How can a believer walk in unforgiveness and not be able to take his/her gifts of prayers to God, or perhaps have a root of bitterness?" This person sounds like a carnal Christian, right? But the Bible teaches that a carnal mind will not and cannot please God (Romans 8:5-8). How can we be ambassadors for Christ when we refuse to do the very act that assured our eternal destiny-forgiveness?

Do you think that people who refuse to forgive will be in that group who will stand before God and say, "Lord, didn't we prophesy in your name, cast out demons, and perform many miracles in your name? and He will answer, I never knew you; depart from me, you who practice lawlessness" (Matthew 7:22-23). Yes, forgiveness is so important that doing it occasionally is not enough. We must commit to a lifestyle of forgiveness.[xxxi] Yes, lifestyle, because forgiveness is core to our new life in Christ; God's forgiveness was revealed in Jesus Christ.

Even after salvation, the Lord made provisions to forgive us because He knew that we would sin and offend others. We also know that even well-meaning Christians offend God and others. If you are around people, it is only a matter of time before you need to forgive and others need to forgive you. Failure to forgive has eternal consequences, which are too important to ignore.

Important principles about forgiveness:
- All of us have frailties and weaknesses.
- We do not deserve forgiveness, but God forgives us.
- Forgiveness does not mean the offense against you was "okay."
- When God forgives you, receive His forgiveness and make sure you forgive yourself and let go of the past.
- Ask God to heal the hurt and give you the grace to forgive others.
- When you hold unforgiveness, you are spiritually tied to the very thing that you hate.

- Forgiveness is setting the other person free so you can also be free. Forgiveness releases both parties.
- Forgiveness is a decision of the will, not an emotion. Feelings will change as you forgive and receive healing of your heart.
- Sometimes, complete forgiveness is a cycle of healing and forgiving. As you forgive as much as you can, you position yourself to receive more healing. As you receive more healing, you will be able to forgive more completely.
- Even if someone purposely hurts us, we still must forgive them from our hearts. If forgiveness is hard for you, keep the desire to forgive before the Lord, and make a decision in your heart to forgive. God will heal you and give you the power to forgive others.
- Forgiveness has the power to heal and set you free from the bondage of bitterness and the pain of your past. Forgiveness will give room in your heart for more love and acceptance from God and others.

Be Available

1 The heavens proclaim the glory of God.
The skies display his craftsmanship.
2 Day after day they continue to speak;
night after night they make him known.
3 They speak without a sound or word;
their voice is never heard.
4 Yet their message has gone throughout the earth,
and their words to all the world. Psalms 19:1

The Lord wants to manifest Himself through his creation. "The heavens declare the glory of God." We are His creation, and He wants to use us to reach His people. He wants to use you, the person He made you, your unique voice, collection of experiences, gifts, abilities, and how you know, love, and understand the Lord.

All through known history, God has chosen to live with us. His desire to be integral in our lives was first realized in the Garden of Eden when God walked in the cool of the day with us.[xxxii] Over thousands of years, God has used many people to get involved in our everyday affairs. We see God in the burning bush reaching out to Moses and in a glory cloud by day and a pillar of fire by night. God was living with them, guiding, leading, protecting and loving.

In recent history, we have seen God coming again to live with us when the Word became flesh and dwelt among us, Jesus Christ. John 1:14

¹⁴ So the Word became human and made his home among us. He was full of unfailing love and faithfulness. And we have seen his glory, the glory of the Father's one and only Son. NLT

God in the flesh again brought forth his plan to live with us physically. Jesus Christ paid our sin debt, so now, by faith in Christ, we have His saving grace to fellowship with Him. Also, through faith (God gave us faith), he created a way to live in us, as the Holy Spirit. Yes, the Spirit of God is currently working in us to transform us into the likeness of his Son, Jesus. Romans 8:28-29

So, the Lord needs you to fully accept his kind and loving plan for eternal life and **love and obey him passionately**. He needs you to:
- Look to Him for help to surrender your right to yourself,
- To resist sin and move from self-centeredness to God's awareness.
- To be open and sensitive to His presence and allow him to live, move and speak through you.

In your everyday life, He wants you to respond to His prompting…to look for Him, and to be honored and excited about being a part of His great plan.

Never forget that God is always at work, everywhere present, redeeming his people. He is, without a doubt, orchestrating His great plan of redemption. He is the beginning and the end. He can see our whole eternal life span. His plan is to unite with us:

- ❖ The priority is salvation; we must connect with God through faith in Jesus Christ:

    8 God saved you by his grace when you believed. And you can't take credit for this; it is a gift from God. 9 Salvation is not a reward for the good things we have done, so none of us can boast about it. 10 For we are God's masterpiece. He has created us anew in Christ Jesus, so we can do the good things he planned for us long ago. Ephesian 2:8-10

- ❖ Secondly, He wants to help us know, understand, and love Him deeply.

    16 I pray that from his glorious, unlimited resources he will empower you with inner strength through his Spirit. 17 Then Christ will make his home in your hearts as you trust in him. Your roots will grow down into God's love and keep you strong. 18 And may you have the power to understand, as all God's people should, how wide, how long, how high, and how deep his love is. 19May you experience the love of Christ, though it is too great to understand fully. Then you will be made complete with all the fullness of life and power that comes from God. Ephesian 3:16-19

- ❖ Live for God and to be available as He prepares us for eternal life with Him.

    13 But we continue to preach because we have the same kind of faith the psalmist had when he said, "I believed in God, so I spoke." 14 We know that God, who raised the

Lord Jesus, will also raise us with Jesus and present us to himself together with you. 15 All of this is for your benefit. And as God's grace reaches more and more people, there will be great thanksgiving, and God will receive more and more glory. 2 Corinthians 4:13-15

❖ His promise is true, Jesus Christ is our hope of glory…

26 the mystery which has been hidden from ages and from generations, but now has been revealed to His saints. 27 To them God willed to make known what are the riches of the glory of this mystery among the Gentiles: which is Christ in you, the hope of glory. 28 Him we preach, warning every man and teaching every man in all wisdom, that we may present every man perfect in Christ Jesus. Colossians 1:26-28

One of the most precious parts of His blessed plan is for God to move through us to reach a hurting and dying world!

Our prayer…Lord, help us to remain available to You.

Giving... God Said Test Me!

"If someone has enough money to live well and sees a brother or sister in need but shows no compassion-how can God's love be in that person?" (1 John 3:17, NLT)

As you read the Gospels, you find that Jesus was moved with compassion because the people were sick, confused, and helpless. It saddened Jesus to see His people hurting because He knows that so many need help, but few are willing to help them (Matthews 9:36). Giving is the "perfect example" of a misunderstood spiritual truth. The enemy has done a good job of blinding our minds, even believers, causing us to forget how important giving is to God. So many needs go unmet because we will not share with others. The scriptural concept of giving is the total opposite of the attitude of this world, with its market-driven message that preaches self-preservation and keeps all you can hoard.

I will admit that it is not natural to give because everything in us fights against giving. The Bible even makes it clear that giving is spiritual; it is an act of your new nature and the Holy Spirit at work. The Bible tells us that the natural person cannot understand spiritual things because it is foolishness to them. (1 Corinthians 2:14). The Word of God warns us not to love money, not to love material things, and not to worry about having our basic needs met. Even believers think that it is okay to spend every waking hour working and going to school to earn more money so that we can spend it on me and mine.

Consequently, we continue to earn more, get more, save more, but not give more. It is not a sin to live well, but it is a sin to be selfish (James 3:16). For this reason, please make sure you share with others so that they can live better, too. It takes faith to give and not worry about whether you will have enough for tomorrow. But a faith that trusts God is essential to pleasing Him.

Giving is the only spiritual truth that God challenges us to test Him. He told us to test Him, right now, on giving to see if it is true (Malachi 3:10)! If He says, I will "supply all of your needs, according to His riches in glory..." He will (Philippians 4:19). Or if He says don't worry about tomorrow, but ask for what you need today, and I will give you enough bread for each day (Matthew 6:11, 25). He also said, I know what you need, so if you ask, I will give you good gifts (Matthew 7:9-11)-hence, agree with God, believe that He is God, and yes, He said to test Him!

Even with a little faith, God is so gracious to bless us. Start giving small amounts-after a while, you will begin to notice that, although you have been giving, you have so much more than you need. You will also notice that your prayers are being answered in ways that fill your heart with joy. He also promised that if you love in deed and in truth, you will receive whatever you ask. (1 John 3:22)

Giving with a joyful heart will cause you to experience what I call "the principle of multiplication," blessings running over until you do not have enough room to store them. But, make sure you share the "running over" portion because when you share the surplus, you will experience the "just because" blessings as well. The "just because blessings" come just because you trusted God and tapped into worship by giving. And yes, there is more! Confidence, peace, joy, and love show up in abundance. And your loved ones become believers, so you have to increase your giving because your cup continues to overflow!

Initially, the act of giving may feel like a duty, but as time passes, you will sense that a partnership of caring emerges. Now, God can trust you with true wealth! The priceless blessings, "true godliness with contentment is itself great wealth" (1 Timothy 6:6). When this happens, you are living a God-pleasing lifestyle, and your only desire is to worship the Lord with your life.

You begin to experience an ease of worship and a singleness of heart to love God with no regrets. You begin to understand the honor of partnering with the Lord to help others because giving is truly a continuation of His love towards us. Indeed, this message started with the importance of giving, and it confirms the love of God and the Spirit of Jesus working through us. But giving is much more significant than it appears. The truth is-we become partners in compassion, extending His reach to His people. How awesome is that? God's blessings are far beyond what we could ever ask or imagine. We give material things, but He gives spiritual blessings, which cannot be compared to any earthly thing!

Rest in the Power of God

This is a spiritual message for your soul!
Question: How do we rest in the Power of God?

> **Hebrews 4:14-16**
> *14 Therefore, since we have a great high priest who has passed through the heavens, Jesus the Son of God, let us hold fast our confession. 15 For we do not have a high priest who cannot sympathize with our weaknesses, but One who has been tempted in all things as we are, without sin.* **16 Therefore let us draw near with confidence to the throne of grace, so that we may receive mercy and find grace to help in time of need.**

Faith is needed in these truths about the sovereign work of God:[xxxiii]
1. You cannot save or sanctify yourself
2. You cannot pay the price for your sin
3. You cannot redeem the world
4. You cannot right what is wrong
5. You cannot purify what is impure
6. You cannot make holy what is unholy

We must have faith in what Jesus Christ has done. He is the perfect atonement for sin. Are you in the habit of regularly acknowledging this truth?

"The greatest need we have is not to do things, but believe things." Oswald Chambers

The redemption of Christ is not just an experience. It is the great act of God, which He has performed through Jesus Christ. AND WE MUST BUILD OUR FAITH ON THIS TRUTH!

Our walk with God should not be based on experiences alone but on the truth about the redemption of Jesus Christ. We should measure our experiences by our Lord Jesus Himself, not by other people. We must build our faith in the redemption of Jesus Christ. We cannot do anything pleasing to God unless we deliberately build on the foundation of the atonement by the Cross of Christ.

> **Hebrews 11:6**
> ⁶ But without faith *it is* impossible to please *Him,* for he who comes to God must believe that He is, and *that* He is a rewarder of those who diligently seek Him.

"The atonement must be shown in practical and humble ways in life. Every time I obey, the absolute deity of God is on my side so that the grace of God and my natural obedience are in perfect agreement." Oswald Chambers

> "Atonement refers to the needed reconciliation between sinful mankind and the holy God. This reconciliation is possible through the atoning sacrifice of Jesus Christ, as expressed in Romans 3:25, Romans 5:11 and Romans 5:19."

Obedience means that I have completely placed my trust in the atonement, and the delight of the supernatural grace of God immediately meets my obedience.

As believers, two of the hardest things for us to do, are to go to Jesus and, secondly, to completely trust in the finished work of the atonement; Jesus declares, Come to Me.

In Mat 11:28-30, the Lord says, Come to Me… And it is hard for us to obey this invitation because we do not trust the supernatural power of the atonement.

Deep down, we know that we must let the Holy Spirit do a work in our hearts before we can go to God. But the Lord continues to stand there with outstretched hands and loving patience and says, Come to Me.

Obedience is the willingness to surrender and to let the Lord work in your heart. So that we can willingly trust in the work of Jesus Christ and have faith in His sovereignty. **We find rest when we:**

- **Believe:** We constantly remember and have faith in the work of Jesus Christ. This is supernatural.
- **Obey:** We completely trust in the redemptive work of the atonement of Christ.
- **Go:** Willing, let the Holy Spirit help us to Come to Jesus, and let Him take our burdens.
- **Rest:** Learn of Christ (spend time) and take on His yoke, which is easy and light.

Matthew 11:28-38
28 Then Jesus said, "Come to me, all of you who are weary and carry heavy burdens, and I will give you rest. 29 Take my yoke upon you. Let me teach you, because I am humble and gentle at heart, and you will find rest for your souls. 30 For my yoke is easy to bear, and the burden I give you is light."

Romans 6:12-14
12 Therefore do not let sin reign in your mortal body so that you obey its lusts, 13 and do not go on presenting the members of your body to sin as instruments of unrighteousness; but present yourselves to God as those alive from the dead, and your members as instruments of righteousness to God. 14 For sin shall not be master over you, for you are not under law but under grace.

2 Peter 1:2-4
*2 Grace and peace be multiplied to you in the knowledge of God and of Jesus our Lord; 3 seeing that **His divine power** has granted to us everything pertaining to life and godliness, through the true knowledge of Him who called us by His own glory and excellence. 4 For by these He has granted to us His precious and magnificent promises, so that by them you may become partakers of the divine nature, having escaped the corruption that is in the world by lust.*

Romans 15:13
*Now, may the **God of** hope fill you with all joy and peace in believing so that you will abound in hope by the **power of the Holy Spirit**.*

In closing, have faith in the work of Jesus Christ, go to God and ask for help. Let us pray for rest in the power of God! Amen

JESUS

I AM With You

"When you go through deep waters, I will be with you. When you go through rivers of difficulty, you will not drown. When you walk through the fire of oppression, you will not be burned up; the flames will not consume you." (Isaiah 43:2, NLT)

"I will be with you," says the Lord God. The Lord made this promise to every major biblical leader, from Abraham to the Apostle Paul. He promised His presence to the children of Israel and to all of us as well. Not only did the Lord promise to be with us, but He also said not to be afraid because He would never leave us or forsake us and that difficulties would not overtake us. (Joshua 1:5) He did not say that we would not have difficulties, but He said when hard times come, do not worry because I AM with you.

As a matter of fact, He tells us that in this life, we will have tribulations, but we must take courage because He has overcome the world. (John 16:33) If I AM is with you, what can harm you? The Lord told Joshua, "No one will be able to stand against you as long as you live." (Joshua 1:5). Many times, in the Bible, God reminds us how much He loves us and we should not worry. Scripture passages from several epistles say to have joy when trials come (James 1:2) because you already know that I am going to cause it to work together for your good. (Romans 8:28)

The Lord God told Moses that His presence would be visible to His people as a cloud by day and a pillar of fire by night. (Exodus 33:14) The Psalmist declares, even if your mother and father forsake you, God will take you up. (Psalms 27:10) Paul wrote in Romans, "that nothing can separate us from the love of God, nothing!" (Romans 8:35-39)

Have you noticed that whenever the Lord gives an assignment, He states not to fear because He is with them? Of course, they were afraid, and we get anxious, too, when God asks us to do something beyond our perceived ability. God does not stop there. He goes on to declare that nobody will hurt you, and the rivers of difficulty or the fire of oppression will not consume you. So, how can I be afraid or despair about anything when I know that God is with me? It is because I am still subject to human frailty and need to call on the Lord for His graciousness to help me overcome fears. Just think about it: the Creator of all things, the whole universe, including us, is with us.

The all-powerful, all-knowing, and everywhere present God is our Father, who chooses to dwell with us. There is something about "knowing" that God is with me that truly gives me so much comfort, a guarantee, and a sense of His living presence. How powerful is this truth that God is always with you? He promises to never leave you nor forsake you! The reality of God's presence is the calming salve of assurance that brings peace and grace to my heart. My self-talk affirms that I am not afraid because God is with me. I can do whatever He told me to do because He is with me. Even in this difficult trial, I will get through it because God is with me. I am hurting and discouraged, but God is with me, so thank

You, Lord, for Your healing touch.

It is God alone who makes a difference in my life. His Presence is not only more than enough; He is enough. Amen!

Jesus - The Christ

Wonderful Counselor, Mighty God-Prince of Peace (Isaiah 9:6).
He is the Lily of the valley (Song of Solomon 2:1). The Bright and Morning Star.
(Rev. 22:16). The Spirit of the LORD is Him - wisdom, knowledge and understanding, counsel, might, and the fear of the Lord. (Isaiah 11:1-3)

He was and is and is to come. (Revelation 1:8)
He was in the beginning, and without Him, nothing would exist. (John 1:1-5)
He is the beginning and the end, Alpha and Omega.
In Him, all things are held together. (Colossians 1:15-20)
He understands our weaknesses because He became flesh and lived among us. (Hebrews 4:14-16, John 1:14)

He is the Fruit of the Spirit-and yes, His fruit is so sweet. (Galatians 5:22-23)
He is love, grace, and hope. And a Savior divine.
A humble King and Worthy Lamb. (Revelation 5:11-13)
He is the great I AM (John 8:57-59).

Holy, Holy, Holy is the Lamb, who came to seek and save the lost. He lived, suffered, and died. He rose with power and glory so that we can have eternal life.
In the end, every knee will bow and every tongue shall confess that Jesus Christ is Lord! (Philippians 2:9-11)

Jesus, Jesus, Jesus, our victorious Savior, and King!

Let this Mind Be In You

For most Christians, Sunday morning is our *Church Day*, and we hear a message, worship in song, have fellowship, and serve each other. During this Lenten season, I am acutely aware of how special it is to fellowship with God through Jesus Christ. And how I could never earn His love nor deserve it; he just loves us. The thought of this truth during praise and worship is overwhelming. As the Psalmist declares, "Such knowledge is too wonderful for me, too great for me to understand!"[xxxiv] I am so grateful for His mercy, love, grace, and kindness!

It is amazing how much easier it is to sense the goodness of God when you go through a time of reflection and confession. Acknowledging the truth about your weaknesses and asking for forgiveness helps us remember how many times we need the forgiveness of God...and how faithful He is to forgive us.[xxxv]

In my faith community, it is called owning your hurt and hurtful behaviors. There is something so right about taking responsibility for yourself and what is wrong. And make sure to give God credit for what is good in your life. God honors our attempts to walk in biblical truth concerning our lives.
We must learn some important spiritual principles as we walk with God. One truth is ensuring that our thoughts about God align with what the bible says about God. For example, the bible says that God only gives good gifts and would never tempt us with evil.[xxxvi] And, of course, we are acutely aware that evil exists in this world, and we live among flawed

people. So, when things go wrong in our lives, we must remember that God does not tempt us with evil; therefore, we should not blame Him.

There are many reasons why things go wrong, but a wise person starts with the possibility that they have contributed to the problem. Of course, not in every situation, but mostly, yes. With that said, we humans tend to be double-minded when it comes to God- we act like He is not there when we "go astray." But we continue to pray to God when we are worried or scared. Usually, these prayers do not come with thankful hearts because we secretly blame God for our troubles. So, let us confess our sins and ask God to cleanse our hearts from ungodly beliefs. The Bible says that we are blessed if we seek God with our whole hearts.[xxxvii]

Too often, we are not convinced that God hears us or is working on our behalf. We usually feel this way because we have not fully accepted the truth about who God is --A great, powerful, all-knowing, everywhere-present God who loves us. God describes Himself as "the Lord who exercises lovingkindness, justice and righteousness on earth..." Jeremiah 9:24

I would submit that we need a little more humility. Humility is almost a dirty word in these modern times. But it is a precious heart attitude encouraged in the Word of God. The Bible says that we should have the mind of Christ, who humbled himself, even to death on the cross.[xxxviii] Humility means I can be wrong and willing to do His will, even if it causes discomfort.

Now, if we could learn how to approach God and life with an openness to loving correction and a hunger for spiritual insight, we would experience much less frustration and more spiritual understanding. This spiritual quality of humility will increase the joy of your salvation and strengthen your faith in God.[xxxix]

Dear Lord, I am awed at your sovereign love towards us. Please continue to give us the mind of Christ, who, although He had spiritual privileges, did not demand comfort or ease of life. Please help me to remember that your ways are perfect.

The Great "I AM"

As I reflect on the bible passages for Lent today, I noticed that they all have a common theme: The Lord is the Great I AM…who is at work in our lives and throughout this world.[xl] He is the creator of life, the author of our salvation and the keeper of promises. Somehow, we seem to forget who is running things in this world. We tend to look to ourselves and others, but the Lord is constantly at work accomplishing His will and purposes for us.

Lord, please forgive us for taking credit for your work, trusting in the works of our hands, and not honoring you as God Almighty. And for not looking to you to help us in our daily lives until problems arise. Then, somehow, we remember to beg you for what we want, and we call that prayer. Lord, you are intimately involved in every aspect of our lives…but we are too self-involved to recognize your presence.

So often, we don't understand life from a spiritual perspective nor live a Spirit-led lifestyle. Romans 8:5-8   We are like children who are not mature enough to understand where their help comes from, as it only comes from the Lord. So, instead of spending so much time doing what we want to do, such as pleasing ourselves and focusing on having fun. Our prayer should be "Lord, please help me trust you more and spend more time with you. Psalms 121:1-3

Lord, all goodness, grace and favor in life comes from you. Today, we acknowledge your great presence and lordship in our lives. Thank you for loving us, protecting us, and just being God. Even though we don't deserve your love, presence, or goodness, you still make provisions for us. Thank you, Lord, we worship you today!

"This is the LORD'S doing; It is marvelous in our sight."
Psalms 118:23

Our Faith

"For whatever is born of God overcomes the world; and this is the victory that has overcome the world-our faith" (1 John 5:4).

Faith in God has the power to transport us from darkness to light and from hopeless sinners to people of God. Putting our faith in Jesus Christ is the most important decision we can make in our lives. God says, "if you confess with your mouth Jesus *as* Lord, and believe in your heart that God raised Him from the dead, you will be saved." (Romans 10:9). We confess and believe that Jesus Christ is our Savior.

Faith in Jesus is what connects us to God and gives us access to eternal life. It is by faith in Jesus Christ that we receive the Holy Spirit and all of the benefits of being a believer. Faith made us partakers of His divine nature (new nature) and gives us all things pertaining to life and godliness; which allows us to escape the lust of this world. (2 Peter 1:3-4) I hear so many church members say, "I'm believing God" for a new car or house or new job. "I'm believing God" to give me a better life, a good church, a great husband, wonderful children, and yes, give me what I want." I have said it, too!

So often, we quote and believe scriptures out of context, like, "Ask what you will and God will give it to you." So, we pray and wait, and pray and wait some more, and when we don't get these tangible things in this material world, we get mad, I mean really mad at God, some even fall away. So many Christians are angry and hard-hearted towards God because they wanted something and did not get it upon demand. (James 4:1-10)

We believe that we have a right to the "good life." The good life is some version of the "American Dream" or some state of living that we think will make us happy. God never promised us the "good life." In fact, Jesus told us that we would have tribulation and this world is not our home. When we became Christians, we gave up the right to ourselves, and now we belong to God. This is a fundamental truth that all believers must surrender to and acknowledge. Jesus taught that if you try to hold on to your life, you will lose it.

Faith is not about "trusting God" to give us what we want. But faith "trusts God" and Him alone. Trusting God means that God is real and He is who He says He is. We miss the part about Him giving us His best. Sadly, many of us do not care to seek His best; we just want what we want because we think we know what is best for us. We do not bother to search the Word of God to understand the meaning of His sovereign power, knowledge, and presence. We want the benefits of being saved from eternal hell but do not want to live according to His principles. We do not want faith to surrender to God or to overcome the world; we want faith to get more. Me, me, self, self is the spirit of the old nature and the carnal mind. Whenever we operate or pray according to our wants, it should be a warning that our attitude and approach to God are self-centered. Having faith in God accepts the truth that He only means us well, and therefore, in the midst of a broken and fallen world, He is moving on our behalf to cause ALL things to work together for our good. When we love God, we are open to His eternal and divine work, which He is doing to accomplish His will for our lives. (Roman 8:28-29)

Circumstances of life are temporary, but His will is eternal. So, we are encouraged to trust God and look to Jesus for grace to live through difficulties, knowing that our Deliverer is always working to help us. The Lord knows that we cannot see the future or even understand why suffering is necessary. That is why He asked us to walk by faith, live by faith, and trust that his good hand is upon us.

Walking by faith means trusting that God is going to accomplish His eternal will in our lives. So, we should acknowledge that we do have His grace, mercy, and peace to surrender to His will and the faith to trust God to overcome the world. Perfect peace comes when we are born of God by faith (new nature), led by the Holy Spirit, and trust that God has overcome the world. "Faith is ALL important in the life and soul of the believer…"

"…but without Faith, there can be no approach to God, no forgiveness, no deliverance, no salvation, no communion, no spiritual life at all." By A.W. Tozer, The Pursuit of God, 1993

God's Rest is a Gift

Pleasing God also means trusting that He knows what is best for us. He gave us the gift of rest -- in the Old Testament, it is called Sabbath, a day to rest because He knew we needed it. He did it for love because He wants the best for us. In the New Testament, just like His Father, Jesus offers us rest...

Matthew 11:28-30
> *"Are you tired? Worn out? Burned out on religion? Come to me. Get away with me, and you'll recover your life. I'll show you how to take a real rest. Walk with me and work with me-watch how I do it. Learn the unforced rhythms of grace. I won't lay anything heavy or ill-fitting on you. Keep company with me, and you'll learn to live freely and lightly."* MSG

He knows we will over-extend ourselves and rely on ourselves more than Him so then we will carry burdens never intended for us and become weary. He knew we would go our way and do what pleases us before choosing the best. He knows that we are but dust and sheep who need a Shepherd.

"We should ask ourselves these questions and ponder the answers: [xli]
- Why are you unwilling to stop for rest?
- Why do you lack faith in this commandment?
- What could you be telling yourself that keeps you resistant toward Sabbath?
- What are you afraid you might hear if you stop?

> "I suspect, as with most of life, it comes down to a need to be wanted/needed/useful/productive that comes out as busyness, and therefore my identity and security is not being centered fully in God."

Why did God ask us to remember the sabbath? Ex 31:12,13. It is a *sign that we belong to God.*

> ***12*** *The* L<small>ORD</small> *spoke to Moses, saying,* ***13*** *"But as for you, speak to the sons of Israel, saying, 'You shall surely observe My sabbaths; for this is a sign between you and Me throughout your generations, that you may know that I am the* L<small>ORD</small> *who sanctifies you.*

When we have a measure of rest in our daily and weekly lives… There is fullness and confidence in knowing that God is with me and that I don't have to fix everything. I sense His presence, and my heart accepts His lordship over Chronos time and all time. An awareness that God is transforming me into the likeness of Christ –I'm not doing it; he is. I'm not working; he is.

God said to remember the Sabbath and don't forget the gift I gave you. It is the answer to our fallen nature that plagues us, enslaves us-and works hard to keep us from knowing God and all of the beauty that comes with resting in Him.

Let's look at the original 4th Commandment: Exodus 20:8-11
> **8** "Remember the sabbath day, to keep it holy. **9** Six days you shall labor and do all your work, **10** but the seventh day is a sabbath of the L<small>ORD</small> your God; *in*

it, you shall not do any work, you or your son or your daughter, your male or your female servant or your cattle or your sojourner who stays with you. **11** For in six days the LORD made the heavens and the earth, the sea and all that is in them, and rested on the seventh day; therefore, the LORD blessed the sabbath day and made it holy.

We must learn how to rest in God because most of us, especially Americans, don't have a tradition of rest. When we did observe the Sabbath, it was typically rigid and legalistic. We have to create our own rhythm of rest. The Sabbath is not just a legalistic act of doing nothing one day per week. It is spending time with God, wanting to be with God, and knowing that God wants to be with us. When we move beyond just wanting it or talking about it but doing it, magical things happen in our lives. Isaiah 58:13-14 shares with us how to approach Sabbath...

> [13] "If because of the sabbath, you turn your foot
> From doing your *own* pleasure on My holy day,
> And call the sabbath a delight, the holy *day* of
> the LORD honorable,
> And honor it, desisting from your *own* ways,
> From seeking your *own* pleasure
> And speaking *your* word,
> [14] Then you will take delight in the LORD,
> And I will make you ride on the heights of the earth;
> And I will feed you *with* the heritage of Jacob your
> father, For the mouth of the LORD has spoken."

Let us end with Hebrews 4:6-11

> "**6** So God's rest is there for people to enter, but those who first heard this good news failed to enter because they disobeyed God. **7** So God set another time for entering his rest, and that time is **today**. God announced this through David much later in the words already quoted:
>
> "Today when you hear his voice,
>   don't harden your hearts."
>
> **8** Now if Joshua had succeeded in giving them this rest, God would not have spoken about another day of rest still to come. **9** So there is a special rest still waiting for the people of God. **10** For all who have entered into God's rest have rested from their labors, just as God did after creating the world. **11** So let us do our best to enter that rest. But if we disobey God, as the people of Israel did, we will fall." NLT

Let us pray…

God help us to rest from our labors… help us to obey your words to enter your rest… Lord, help me to trust you and do your will, to come to you and rest…

The Beginning of Wisdom

"The fear of the LORD is the beginning of wisdom and knowledge of the Holy One is understanding" (Proverbs 9:10 NIV).

Wisdom comes from God, and it starts with fear (reverence). To know about God is to understand His eternal nature, His supernatural power, His holy presence, and His all-knowing gaze. He is the Creator of all things, including us. He has a purpose and plan for each of us. Accordingly, it is "wise" to agree with God. If you know about His power, you know what He can do (Matthew 10:28-29).

But the Bible also tells us that "perfect love casts out fear…" (1 John. 4:18), which tells me that there is more to understanding God. There is a perfect love that has no fear. I pondered this scripture for a long time because, at that time, I did not understand what it meant. I thought, *"Lord, I'm a Christian, but I'm still afraid that I will mess up and lose your love."* This cannot be the love described in the Word of God, "…fear has torment." Likewise, there is no place for torment in love.

Well, what did I fear, what tormented me? My greatest fear was that I might fall out of favor with God because when I found out many years ago that God is real–I was also painfully aware that I did not deserve His love. I was so scared of missing the mark with God. This caused constant confession of sins and repentance from my wicked ways. I spent many years serving in the ministry until I worked myself to exhaustion because "I" tried to stay right with God in my own strength as if this was something I could do on my own! I was a believer for many years but continued to carry the guilt and the burden of sin. I was afraid to let go and depend on God. I did not know how to trust Him. I knew about His saving grace without really understanding biblical salvation.

I was afraid of God because I was not at a place in my walk with God to know the truth about His liberty. Neither did I have a context for being free from fear because most of my life consisted of being afraid, overlooked, and disappointed. These lifelong feelings shaped my existence and motivated me to be well-behaved and responsible. I was careful not to mess up my life or make poor decisions that would harm my family and friends. It took years after salvation to learn how to rest in the gracious love of God.

I'm still learning the scope of His love, but now I know in my innermost being that God loves me without condition. He will never leave me nor forsake me. Trusting God is like floating on water; you cannot float if you do not completely let go, relax, and rest in Him. I missed the WHOLE point of the gospel. If we could live a sin-free life and earn favor, why did Jesus need to die? His atonement for our sin and redemptive work on the cross demonstrates that perfect love.

We don't have to be afraid of God or think He is going to hurt us because His nature is love. He had already shown His loving intention when He sacrificed His best when we were at our worst. This is love without fear!

So now, you don't have to worry about earning His love or being punished by God. Since He already loves us, we can be free to love and trust God. Trust is an unwavering confidence in His love and acceptance of us. He loves me now and forever! Knowing Him as expressed through Jesus Christ is love perfected.

"But the wisdom from above is first of all pure. It is also peace loving, gentle at all times, and willing to yield to others. It is full of mercy and the fruit of good deeds. It shows no favoritism and is always sincere. [18] And those who are peacemakers will plant seeds of peace and reap a harvest of righteousness." (James 3:17-18 NLT).

To Know Him is To Love Him:
"And may you have the power to understand, as all God's people should, how wide, how long, how high, and how deep his love is. [19] May you experience the love of Christ, though it is too great to understand fully. Then you will be made complete with all the fullness of life and power that comes from God." (Ephesians 3:18-19 NLT)

Faith Believes Him: [3] By faith we understand that the entire universe was formed at God's command, that what we now see did not come from anything that can be seen. (Hebrew 11:3) "For I can do everything through Christ, who gives me strength." (Philippians 4:13)

Understanding Reveals Him: "Those who accept my commandments and obey them are the ones who love me. And because they love me, my Father will love them. And I will love them and reveal myself to each of them." (John 14:21)

Love Receives Him and Loves Him who loved us first:

"Jesus replied, "What does the law of Moses say? How do you read it?" *²⁷ The man answered, " 'You must love the Lord your God with all your heart, all your soul, all your strength, and all your mind.' And, 'Love your neighbor as yourself." ²⁸ "Right!" Jesus told him. Do this and you will live!" (Luke 10:26-28)*

True Riches

"The Lord is my Shepherd; I shall not want." (Psalm 23:1)

So many messages bombard our minds about wanting more. We think, "I need a new car, more clothes, and shoes, etc. I would be happier if I lived in a bigger house," or, "If only my husband was more sensitive." Not to mention flawed, "religious" messages that suggest that having possessions determines God's love for you or that our lack of things means something is wrong with our faith. Unfortunately, we agree with viewpoints that contradict God's Word and we become frustrated because we do not have more things, more money, more vacations, more, more and more. The Word of God says, do not love this world (1 John 2:15).

Contentment comes from the truth of God. God is our Shepherd. He loves, protects, and meets all of our needs according to His riches. God's riches have more to do with spiritual than material things. The Bible says, "… the kingdom of God is not eating and drinking, but righteousness and peace and joy in the Holy Spirit." (Romans 14:17)

God's riches are eternal life, the written Word, and the indwelling Holy Spirit. The Holy Spirit guides, instructs, comforts, and leads us. His Word confirms that we belong to God, and His grace and mercy are available to us every day. The Holy Spirit makes us new and gives gracious gifts and the power not to sin. We have peace with God and peace we cannot explain and the added bonus of joy, which is our strength.

So, the question still remains: have you embraced God's true riches? Why do you discount your God-given inheritance and fret over material things and cares of this world? It is true that material things are needed to live and we need enough to keep us honest. But make sure they are in their rightful place in your heart. Please do not allow the care for material things to prevent you from experiencing a vibrant, joy-filled love life with the Lord. The Bible declares that godly contentment is great gain! You might reply, "But what about my wayward children and my spouse not being saved?" God's response is to trust Him with your children and family. "Cast your cares upon Him because he cares for you" (1 Peter 5:7).

God promised and is faithful to give you enough grace to get you through every challenge. The Bible tells us to renew our minds, seek the Lord, and think on things that are good and honorable. "Don't worry, but pray with thanksgiving. God's peace will guard your hearts and minds" (Philippians 4:6-7). This is Truth- God gives us everything pertaining to life and godliness (2 Peter 1:3a).

Our destiny includes eternal life in heaven and abundant life with God on earth. So, let us stop the "I want more" madness and embrace His true riches. Have joy when trials come and your faith gets tested because you grow in patience, which produces completeness and the awareness that we have no lack (James 1:2-5).

Understand trials as an opportunity for growth and declare without hesitation, The Lord is enough… "I shall not want" (Psalm 23:1b).

Truth That Transforms

This is the story- I want to be good for God. But I wasn't asking God to "help" me to be good for Him. I felt that it was my responsibility to be a mature and responsible Christian. After all, I have been a believer for some decades, and the Lord has already given me so much, just to name a few gifts: salvation, love, mercy, forgiveness, grace, and the ever-present Holy Spirit. Oh, and do not forget some joy and peace, too.

This is pride- Frustrated and disappointed with my human frailties drove me quietly away from being available to God or seeking Him with my whole heart. I knew that the Lord was speaking, but I would not come close enough or quiet myself to hear Him. Ministry duties caused me to seek Him for help with a message or how to counsel someone, but there was no regular intimate communion with Him. My heart had strayed because I was trying to do His will on my own. I grew tired of trying to hear from the Lord or setting special times for intimacy. Also, I was very weary because of some struggles in life. There were many difficult realities regarding friends and family that hurt me deeply. So often, I wished that I did not care so much so I would not hurt so much. That feeling of not wanting to care about others was a clear sign that I was not in a healthy place and that I was focusing too much on the burden of love and not on the power of love.

The deep pain of life was when my son became very ill (again) and stayed in the hospital twice for fourteen days over two months. These episodes caused much fear and uncertainty, and they were a reminder that in spite of my great love for my son, I could not fix him. I could not heal him nor shield his wife and children from the trauma and fear of losing a husband and father. I was so angry, and I needed relief from the pain of it all. So, I went back to God begging for help. Of course, He helped me because He is love.

He gave me a powerful word of encouragement...And then I had an A HA moment! I had flawed thinking! I thought I should not need God so much! I was so wrong! The Lord is strong in our weaknesses.

The truth that transforms- I was prompted by God to accept the constant reality of being a fragile human. (2 Corinthians 12:7-10) My confessions to God about how I really felt gave me additional relief, and the acknowledgement that I was so frail caused me to ask for help again and again. At every request, I found grace and mercy, which is His ability and strength to get me through that moment or day. Now, this process has the potential for sustainability. Praise the Lord!

But the Lord had a few questions for me. Why is it so hard for you to depend on Me? Who said you had to be good for Me? Did I tell you that you had to be mature and responsible in your own strength? As a child, you learned to deal with pain and trauma by shielding your heart and taking care of those you loved. This auto response has shaped your life. God reminded me, "Although there were brief moments of needing Me- You defaulted back to trying to please Me and others by not depending on Me for help but by trying to prove to Me (and others) that you are a good person because you were self-sufficient." Independence is a type of idolatry (self-worship) and an offense to God. None of us are good, only Jesus is good. Jesus died and rose because we were not able to "be good."

The right thinking flooded my mind: *you were raised and taught not to bother others or the Lord.* "But I am the only One Who can help you, heal you, and use you for My purposes. I help you because I love you with everlasting love. On occasion, when you accepted My help, you would tell others about it because you wanted to impress them with your connection with me, your "spirituality." You wanted to be respected as a "healer," "wise one," or the one who has a "special" relationship with Me-a sage.

Many times, you have taken credit for what only I can do. Yes, I use (anoint) you to reach my people. But can I use you (to show my love) when you are offended, inconvenienced, or attacked? What about allowing Me to love your enemies or the unlovable? Are you available to Me? Can I use you to love them like I love you?" (Matthew 5:11; John 15; 1 John 4:7-21)

"Okay, Lord- No, I do not have to try so hard to be good or mature for You. With You, I can be a child: dependent, weak, silly, immature, carefree, selfish, amazed, and joyful. I can believe and be needy, and I do not have to fix anything. There is no pressure to perform. All I need to do is just let You move and do what only You can do. Lord, forgive me for living according to a lie that I should not need You so much. Help me, Lord, to always sanctify You as Lord in my heart." (1 Peter 3:15)

This is the truth about the fallen nature- We want to be God. We want to take credit for the things that only God can do. We want to impress people with the gifts and qualities that only come from God. We want people to be impressed with us. We are people pleasers, not God pleasers.

God's message to me- "Yes, I have called you to wisdom, My Wisdom, I named you Wise Discerner," says the Lord. "I gave you the motivational gifts[xlii] of perception (insight), wisdom, and My truth, which transforms. BUT I OPERATE BEST in a vessel that is yielded and dependent on Me. I will CONTINUE to help you cast yourself (cares) upon Me, trust Me, love Me, and learn how to respond to Me as a loving daughter, My daughter." Amen!

A Message for Life

His Goodness, Mercy, and Presence

Only God can give rest for your soul, peace in hard times and hope amidst disappointments. Only He can heal a broken heart, give power to forgive and set us free from burdens and bitter failures in this fallen world--And, most importantly, give us eternal life through faith in Jesus Christ. This message is being shared to reflect His desire to commune with us as we experience His lovingkindness. The essence of His presence and the power of His truth will answer our questions-address our struggles, fulfill His purpose, and give us joy in this life.

So often, when difficulties arise, we turn to family, friends and loved ones, but God wants us to turn to Him first! God wants us to deal with our challenges and disappointments as we seek His face-And trust that He only means us well and His intentions are kind. Walking in His abiding love will impact how we live, make decisions, and respond to God and others. Only when we decide (an act of our will) to believe with our whole heart that God sincerely loves us and we embrace the deep reservoir of His love can we understand His expansive love, experience His abiding presence, and have the confidence of knowing Him.

In recent years, the Lord revealed that many of us have a divided heart. We think our hearts are whole, but we have sections that are closed to God. Have you ever wondered how you can be loving towards God, sense his presence, and do His will? And almost at the same time, have dark thoughts, wonder if God is there and can willfully sin. I suggest that we have natural defense mechanisms that are on automatic pilot. But these defense mechanisms have done their job too well.[xliii] I pray that we all learn how to let His kind intention towards us be a transformative expression of intimate communion with the Father and His Son, Jesus Christ.

There was a season in my life when I realized that I was exhausted -- physically, emotionally, and spiritually. Let me share a VERY brief summary of the first 35 years of walking with the Lord:

- Accepted the Lord Jesus Christ as Lord and Savior, happy and excited about being saved and part of the faith community
- Joined church and became a faithful member, serving God with all my might. But in reality, I lived a life of spiritual highs/lows, on fire for the Lord, faithfully serving in ministry, on the one hand, but painfully aware of ongoing failures and character weaknesses that I could not overcome.
- I was always taught (or thought) that after salvation, it was **my** responsibility to have faith, be a good Christian, mortify the flesh, stir up the gifts, serve the Lord, bear good fruit, love everybody, even my enemies and represent God's love in my life. Not just any love, but love like Jesus loves me…
- Don't forget to be humble, forgive and bear one another's burdens. Oh yeah, fight the good fight of faith, put on the whole armor of God, and stand against the wiles of the devil, "casting down every

imagination that exalted itself against the knowledge of Christ" (2 Corinthians 10:4-5).
- And... we must confess our sins, repent, and experience His cleansing and refreshing. Ensure you have a consistent prayer, praise, and worship life, be a good steward, mother, wife, and friend, and remember to give to the poor.
- Oh, do not forget Bible study, daily devotion, and faithfully giving to the work of the ministry.

I tried to do all of the above for many years, but something was missing –There was too much self-appointed effort, sacrifice and busyness. There were too many religious activities and not enough grace. Life with God wasn't supposed to be so heavy, hard, or so much effort without some joy, lightness, or peace.

I needed a Word from the Lord, so I asked Him for help. He answered and revealed that I was not looking to Him enough for help nor trusting or resting in Him. Neither was there enough faith nor understanding about the benefits we all have in the new life in Christ, which includes Jesus' promise to lift our heavy burdens. Jesus said, "Come to Me and learn of Me. My yoke is easy, and My burden is light." (Mat. 11:29-30) What great news! So, I asked the Lord to please help me to understand His message of trust and grace. As I spent quiet time with the Lord, three biblical principles emerged in my heart:
- We cannot do His will without His grace.
- His grace is always available to believers who need it, want it, and walk in it.

- He gives us grace to get what we need from Him. We need His grace to get His grace.

If you do not understand these three principles, you will miss the precious message of grace. And you will not experience a life free from the tyranny of our stubborn nature. Our new life in Christ is a life of grace. The Lord offers us a continual supply of grace. "For sin shall not be master over you, for you are not under law but under grace" (Romans 6:14). Sin (fallen nature) is not my master; it does not control me!

God's grace is available to help me live according to His will. What is grace? Grace is more than the typically quoted definition of undeserved favor. Grace is a gift from God, including His love for us and enabling power to transform our lives. We activate this sufficient grace through faith. The same faith it took to believe in God for salvation is the faith needed to trust Him to work in us. We must learn to "know" (full confidence by faith) that His grace is (right now) available to us (Hebrews 4:14-16).

Faith is the critical link between God and us. We were saved by faith and received the Holy Spirit by faith (Galatians 3:2). Confident trust in His loving presence (His desire to help you) and the dependence on Him (accept His help to surrender your will) …is what releases His sufficient grace in your life. "My grace is sufficient for you; My power is perfected in weakness…" (2 Corinthians 12:9). When we acknowledge His grace, we understand that… Asking Him is an act of faith… Requesting His help is our acknowledgment that we are weak and need Him…Surrendering is to yield, not to our will, but to God's will. And finally, requesting that God would do what only God can do. Casting our cares, self-will, self-efforts, and divided hearts upon the Lord –and being open to accepting His will as we respond with trust and loving obedience- is what positions us to walk in the **fullness** of His grace. When we struggle with yielding, it usually involves being double-minded: I want God in my life but still want to be in control. My heart wants to love and trust God fully, but it also wants to protect its right to self-will….

The Bible describes double-mindedness as unstable, like waves, tossed to and fro, this means we cannot receive anything from God (James 1:6-8). You cannot serve the world (self) and God. God can only be the Lord of your life. We are not equal with God; He is not an idol made by hands. Double-mindedness is a barrier to connecting with the Lord. But if we pray and ask for help, God will help us trust only in Him and give us the grace to become single-minded and love Him wholeheartedly.

Although walking in the fullness of God's grace is a life-long journey, the Lord provides His grace to have faith in His saving grace and to walk in His sufficient grace.[xliv]

The scriptural prayer for our life is Ephesians 3:14-19:*14 When I think of all this, I fall to my knees and pray to the Father, 15 the Creator of everything in heaven and on earth. 16 I pray that from his glorious, unlimited resources he will empower you with inner strength through his Spirit.*

17 Then Christ will make his home in your hearts as you trust in him. Your roots will grow down into God's love and keep you strong. 18 And may you have the power to understand, as all God's people should, how wide, how long, how high, and how deep his love is. 19May you experience the love of Christ, though it is too great to understand fully. Then you will be made complete with all the fullness of life and power that comes from God. NLT

My Confession

I think about this season of spiritual correctness during reflection and repentance. I am reminded of the many times I did not approach life God's way. A perfect example is when, instead of wanting to please God and prefer others, I just wanted to do things my way, which was convenient for me. Even the bible says, love God first; love others, just like you love yourself. Unfortunately, I did not love others as much as I love myself. Although I try to be kind and considerate, as a "good" Christian should, my consideration of others is limited by what I consider too much.

The sin is not that I do not do enough or could do more. The sin is that in my heart, I do not care to consider how God would have me treat others. I often did not want to pray, seek advice, or even ponder whether my actions were from a place of love. (1 Cor 13) Agape love is a love that comes with grace and goes beyond our human capacity. But, of course, I did not want to follow that path because it might require more from me than I was willing to give. Well, herein lies the problem: as a Christian, I have dishonored one of God's most important biblical principles, which is sharing God's love.

"For God, so loved the world, that He gave…" And God gave His best, "His one and only Son." Jesus was not concerned about His comfort or suffering for all humankind as inconvenient! While on earth, He did not walk in His heavenly privileges to ease His pain of life.

Our Savior came as a humble servant and lived a difficult and sacrificial life that included death on the cross "so that whoever believes in Him, would not perish, but shall have eternal life." John 3:16

What does this have to do with me? As a Christian, I am a benefactor of His great love. And therefore, His great love comes with a mandate to share His love with others. Likewise, eternal life is a gift of love and comes with His grace to help us love our neighbors –We know that loving others requires more than just thinking nice thoughts. Love is an action verb. Genuine love includes giving time and effort.

Being a recipient of God's love obligates us to love Him and our neighbors. He even put His love in our hearts so that we can experience it and share it with others. "His love has been shed abroad in our hearts and if our hearts fail us, God says that He is greater than our hearts… 1 John 3:20

Dear Lord, forgive me for not wanting to be inconvenienced. Please give me the desire to say yes to your will and purpose. Thank you for your great mercy and willingness to forgive me.

PRAYER

Resist Evil - Warfare is Essential

Spiritual warfare is not optional for believers of our Lord and Savior Jesus Christ. It is essential in resisting and guarding against evil. And although we must fight for the protection and the spiritual well-being of others, we are not fighting people. Our battles are not against people but spiritual darkness and wickedness in this world.

It is easy to forget that our battle is spiritual when people come against us, mistreat, and try to hurt us, right? We get angry and upset at people, but it is the influence of evil that causes harm to you and your loved ones. The Bible teaches that there is an evil presence in this world. And that Satan, sometimes called the Devil, is the prince of this world. So, it is important to understand and believe that evil exists. There is so much that we don't understand about the unseen spiritual world. But the bible gives us strategies that we can employ to resist and guard against evil.

Of course, knowing that our fight is spiritual is central to warfare. So, we need to ensure we use spiritual weapons for spiritual battles.[xlv] You cannot bring carnal weapons to a spiritual battle! Trying to address spiritual matters with natural methods can lead to feelings of failure, defeat, and discouragement. Many believers even stop reading the Bible and going to church. But the Bible teaches us not to get discouraged. Since the true work of God is eternal and unseen, and what we see in this world is temporary. So, as we trust God, we know He is faithful to complete His good work in us.[xlvi]

As we prepare our minds and attitudes to be more than conquerors in Him who loved us…Jesus Christ.[xlvii] We must study **what the bible teaches about how to fight.** The battle is spiritual, and warfare involves many prayer battles that are fought simultaneously. To be successful in spiritual warfare, we must practice some biblical rules of engagement. Let us start with the teaching from James 4:7: **"Submit therefore to God. Resist the devil, and he will flee from you."** Having a yielded heart before the Lord gives us the power to resist evil.

God has set some rules of engagement that we may not fully understand. And there is much about the spiritual world that we know very little about, and very few people are granted access to spiritual awareness and insight. So, we must follow biblical teachings. For example, the spiritual world is stratified by hierarchy and ranking. And we should never fight above our rank. Our spiritual ranking is similar to our natural ranking. Unless God has called you to a special prayer and spiritual warfare assignment, be careful to pray directly to the Lord to resist and bind evil. If we break these rules of engagement, it may cause needless casualties of war.[xlviii] Accordingly, you should look to God to make sure you are not breaking spiritual warfare rules. When we pray, we ask the Lord to resist the enemy's work in the name of Jesus Christ. And ask the Lord to cover and protect your loved ones from evil and bind the work of evil. We should always look to the Lord to fight our spiritual and life battles.

As you engage in spiritual battles for others, you must be aware of your spiritual fitness, as the enemy will try to attack you and others simultaneously. Our spiritual fitness will help us to be formable in battle. The enemy does not fight fair and will try to divide and conquer. The enemy will try to distract you from praying while trying to cause others to make harmful decisions.

Our spiritual fitness involves wearing God's full armor, which is available to us. This armor includes spiritual weapons we need to fight. Let us look at what the Word of God says in Ephesians 6:10-18:

> **10** A final word: Be strong in the Lord and in his mighty power. **11** Put on all of God's armor so that you will be able to stand firm against all strategies of the devil. **12** For we are not fighting against flesh-and-blood enemies, but against evil rulers and authorities of the unseen world, against mighty powers in this dark world, and against evil spirits in the heavenly places.
>
> **13** Therefore, put on every piece of God's armor so you will be able to resist the enemy in the time of evil. Then after the battle you will still be standing firm. **14** Stand your ground, putting on the belt of truth and the body armor of God's righteousness. **15** For shoes, put on the peace that comes from the Good News so that you will be fully prepared. **16** In addition to all of these, hold up the shield of faith to stop the fiery arrows of the devil. **17** Put on salvation as your helmet, and take the sword of the Spirit, which is the word of God. **18** Pray in the Spirit at all times and on

every occasion. Stay alert and be persistent in your prayers for all believers everywhere.

It is clear from these scriptures that God wants us to stand our ground using His spiritual weapons of truth, the gospel, righteousness, and faith, to name a few. Trusting God and staying connected to Him in prayer helps us to stay strong. Before Nehemiah made preparation to fight, in chapter 4:4, he prayed to God...And in verse 15 it says, and God frustrated their (enemy) plans...Daniel 11:32b says that the people who know their God shall be strong and carry out *great exploits.*

Yes, the full armor of God is the weapon needed to fight spiritual battles in prayer...but then there is more! Our lifestyle should reflect our love for God and His plan.

- Be fully confident and agree with what Jesus Christ says about you... I am more than a conqueror through Christ Jesus. I can do all things through Christ who strengthens me.[xlix] Jesus told us that, ⁵I am the vine, you are the branches; he who abides in Me and I in him, he bears much fruit, for apart from Me you can do nothing.[l]

- We should walk in the truth of God's word and live according to His will.

- We should refuse to entertain thoughts that do not follow God's Word. "We destroy every proud obstacle that keeps people from knowing God. We capture their rebellious thoughts and teach them to obey Christ."[li]

- We must forgive, even have a lifestyle of forgiveness. Forgiveness is another gift that allows you to get freed from the bondage of your past and live free to love God and others. I can't say enough about forgiveness…

- Prayer is our connection to God and a powerful weapon in our arsenal. Hebrews 4:16 says that we can go boldly to the throne of grace to receive mercy and find grace to help in times of need.

- The joy of the Lord is our strength… choose joy. It is a gift from God!

- Walk in the peace of God, which surpasses understanding and will guard your heart and mind.[lii]

- Having the mind of Christ is a weapon against evil; walk humbly before the Lord.[liii]

Ultimately, the victory belongs to the Lord, and we are overcomers because He is our Great Captain. He is the Lord of Host! According to the Word of God in Philippians 2:10-11:

> **10** that at the name of Jesus, every knee should bow, in heaven and on earth and under the earth,
> **11** and every tongue declare that Jesus Christ is Lord, to the glory of God the Father.

Please remember what the Lord says: His grace is sufficient for whatever we are going through! His strength is made perfect in our weaknesses.[liv] Finally, we support our loved ones by loving them and giving wise counsel, resources, and a godly foundation. Never forget that the true deliverer is the lover of our souls and the only one who can help us and our families --The Lord God Almighty!

Believe God and live like you trust what His word promises – and you will be a mighty warrior for the Lord and a great protector of your family and community.

What Hinders Our Prayers?

Prayer and the Golden Rule

[7] "Ask, and it will be given to you; seek, and you will find; knock, and it will be opened to you. [8] For everyone who asks receives, and he who seeks finds, and to him who knocks it will be opened. [9] Or what man is there among you who will give him a stone when his son asks for a loaf? [10] Or if he asks for a fish, he will not give him a snake, will he? [11] If you then, being evil, know how to give good gifts to your children, how much more will your Father who is in heaven give what is good to those who ask Him! [12] "In everything, therefore, treat people the same way you want them to treat you, for this is the Law and the Prophets. Matthew 7:7-12

This scripture compares an earthly parental relationship with a heavenly one. So, we assume that just like a father provides for his children, God will, too. But let's look at this scripture a little closer.

1. There is a covenant relationship between the father and the son.
2. They are correctly related in terms of each person doing what is expected in that relationship:
    a. The son honors and obeys his father
    b. The father cares and provides for his son
    c. The son asked the father for bread and fish, which are referred to as good gifts (what they need and what the father is supposed to give)

3. The previous three verses talk about asking, seeking, and knocking…Asking who, God? In other words, this scripture suggests that you have to be in a relationship with God, in covenant: Father God and son/daughters
4. **Asking** a certain way (by faith with thanksgiving), **seeking** God with your yielded heart and knocking, requesting entry to His presence
5. Every covenant relationship has some basic rules, principles, expectations, etc.
6. Of course, our covenant relationship with God begins with faith in Jesus Christ,
7. However, there is a big difference between being a baby in the Lord and a son or daughter

So, the question we would like to explore in this passage:

Are you a good child asking God for good things?

In the attitude of your heart…Do you recognize God and our Lord Jesus Christ as all-powerful, all-knowing, and everywhere present? What about His lovingkindness, justice, and holiness?

Do you accept that God loves you, and do you love him back? So, loving God should be demonstrated (at least) in the following ways:
- Your love is expressed by your willingness to depend on Him to help you do His will, knowing that you cannot do his will without Him. (Draw near to Him and surrender)[lv]
- You submit your whole life to Him with worship and love. Give your life as a living sacrifice, holy and acceptable.[lvi]

Covenant with God involves holiness (meaning exclusively surrendered), love and forgiveness[lvii]. And agree with His ways and His will (obey). And to spend every season of your life seeking after God, which leads to several things that God asks of us:
- Know and understand the Lord (word, will and ways), assemble, be lights in the world, practice godly living, make disciples, spend time with Him, serve the Lord with gladness, confess your sins and finally, love, forgive and be kind to others.

Are you a good child asking God for good things?
Just in case you need more specific examples of a good relationship with the Lord. I have a few more questions for you to ponder as you think about your prayer life and being in covenant with God:
- Are you mean and hard to get along with?
- Do you owe money to God and others?
- Do you have unforgiveness in your heart?
- Are you judgmental or critical of others?
- Are you envious of or jealous when others are blessed or doing well?
- Do you trust God? Do you believe that God is in control and nothing is impossible for Him?
- Do you believe that God is punishing you when times are hard? Or do you believe that nothing can separate you from the love of God?
- Are you submitted to God? Do you resist evil?
- Do you desire to please Him?
- Are you resisting God when you know that the Lord gave you clear instructions?

- Do you have secret sins? Are you struggling with the lust of the eyes, the lust of the flesh or the pride of life?
- Are you holding back on God? Are you too concerned about what people think?
- Do you ask God regularly to show you areas that need confession?
- Do you practice casting your cares upon the Lord? Do you take your burdens to the Lord? Are you learning from Jesus how to live your life with His yoke?
- Do you take time to quiet yourself, listen to God and practice solitude and silence before the Lord?

Our Father, who art in heaven. Hallowed be thy name. Teach us how to pray according to your will…help us to know how to pray unhindered prayers. To know and understand your will and your ways. May we be enlightened by your loving and refreshing presence in the name of Jesus Christ, our Lord.

We Must Pray

Prayer is such a fundamental part of our Christian life. Prayer is vital and a top priority, as is reading His word or worshiping the Lord. In the NASB version, the word prayer is mentioned **362 times** in the bible. This means prayer is essential to our relationship and walk with the Lord.

Pray without ceasing is a heart that prays with an attitude of prayer and an ongoing belief that we need God. According to the scriptures, we can do nothing without Him[lviii] (we cannot do His will without Him). We need God…

1 Thessalonians 5:16-18 (NASB)
> *[16] Rejoice always; [17] pray without ceasing; [18] in everything give thanks; for this is God's will for you in Christ Jesus.*

Proverbs 14:12
> ***There is a way*** *which seems right to* ***a man****, but its end* ***is*** *the* ***way*** *of death.*

Matthew 7:14
> *For the gate is small and the* ***way*** *is* ***narrow*** *that leads to life, and there are few who find it.*

Luke 18:1 **(NKJV)**
> *Then He spoke a parable to them, that men always ought to pray and not lose heart.*

Prayer is a two-way form of communication, actually it's three ways: us to God, God to us and Holy Spirit to God.[lix] The heart of prayer includes a soul mostly focused on God and His will. When we pray, we ask for direction, seek His will, cast our cares upon Him, and wait for His prompting. A heart that wants to please God with faith and yearns to experience His presence is a heart that is a delight to the Lord. Faith, humility, thankfulness, and love are integral when we pray to the Lord God.

Faith declares that I am fully confident that you can do the impossible. And because of your mercy towards us, I can come to you confidently, knowing that I will receive mercy and grace in need.[lx] If you loved me when I was a sinner, I know you love me now that the blood of Jesus covers me.[lxi]

Humility knows that I truly do not deserve your love and forgiveness. And without the presence of the Holy Spirit in my life, I cannot live as a new creature in Christ Jesus. Because of you, I can love, obey, and live a life that honors you. We have all sinned and come short of your glory.[lxii] And you are no respecter of persons. Lord, I always need to confess my known and unknown sins because you are faithful in forgiving me. Even with your love, grace, and Holy Spirit, I can still fall short. I swear to my own hurt and confess my sins to you, Lord.[lxiii]

Thankfulness confirms that I cannot fathom your love, grace, mercy, and power. I do not deserve it, but yet you gave it to me. With a grateful heart, I honor you with my life. This knowledge is too wonderful for me.[lxiv] Thank you, thank you, thank you...

Love states that I can only love you, Lord, because you loved me first. Help me, Lord, to fully accept your love until it changes me, and I love you back and love myself, others, and my enemies. I want to do your will because I love you. Not because I am supposed to but because I want to demonstrate my love by doing what pleases you. Lord, I give you all my life, time, dreams, and treasures. I need your direction to know which way to go.

Prayer is also God speaking to us as we listen to Him. The more we quiet ourselves in silence to hear His voice, the more we become accustomed to hearing His voice. The Bible states that you will know His voice and not follow a stranger.[lxv] Therefore, a healthy prayer life is based on the Word of God and a heart condition that embraces:
1. A love relationship with a grateful heart.
2. An attitude that acknowledges the need for God.
3. A heart that is willing to spend time with God.
4. A heart that wants to do life God's way because His way is the only way that leads to life.[lxvi]
5. A heart that will wait quietly and listen for the voice of God and do what He says.[lxvii]
6. We need faith in God that goes beyond our limited notions of who God is, His vast greatness, power, and perfection.[lxviii]
7. Finally, we need a genuine acceptance of His love and kind intention towards us and our love for Him, which cannot be described in words.

Prayer

11 Therefore we also pray always for you that our God would count you worthy of this calling, and fulfill all the good pleasure of His goodness and the work of faith with *power, **12** that the name of our Lord Jesus Christ may be glorified in you, and you in Him, according to the grace of our God and the Lord Jesus Christ. 2 Thessalonians 1:11-12*

We look to you, Lord. Amen

Prayer Against Double-Mindedness

"Love not the world, neither the things that are in the world." (1 John 2:15)

Dear Lord, help me to stop being attracted to worldly things. Show me what I should renounce and reject. Help me to develop these spiritual disciplines of simplicity, silence, solitude, and surrender.[lxix] Guide my days. May I give You the first fruits of my life as I depend on You to make my path straight. Simplify my time, days, weeks, my whole life. Give us direction concerning the next steps. I want to enjoy being with You more than anything else. Help me check my motives. May I give You joy and honor Your name as I live, knowing that You are the most precious Person in life.

To know the truth and live the truth... Lord, help me to live the truth You have already taught me. I cannot love the world and You at the same time. I should love You and reject the world. Oh, how double-minded am I. I reject the lust of the eyes and flesh and the boastful pride of life (1 John 2:16).

Natural things are not evil, but how I want them is the problem. I need to stop longing for things and learn to be content because longing is lusting. Help me not to lust but to be satisfied with You. Help me, Lord, to trust You. What really motivates my heart? I need to have a grateful heart. Only You know, Lord. I repent for my lack of discipline. Help me stay focused on You, Lord.

Prayer for Help

Dear Lord, I look to You and seek You today. Please incline Your ear to me. I'm seeking You with all of my heart (Jeremiah 29:12-14). I'm so tired of being concerned about when I should go. But I will stay and finish my course regarding my present assignment. I will not move until You release me.

Lord, I desire to do Your will and not mine. Give me strength, mercy, and grace to keep my hands and heart towards the things You have entrusted to me. My heart being open to You is my desire. I choose to obey, love, honor, and trust You.

My Lord and Savior fill me with Your Holy Spirit and give me the grace to walk humbly before You.

Prayer of Confession

Lord, please forgive me for being so critical, judgmental, and even hypocritical. I was critical towards someone because they were struggling with an issue for many years. I was reminded that I have struggled with weight and other issues for many years as well.

Lord, I renounce my self-righteous attitude. I repent. Help me, Lord, to be more genuine and keep me aware of the darkness that tries to invade my life. Help me to stay in Your light. Fill my heart with Your love. Only You can show us the real truth about the condition of our hearts.

Thank You, Lord

Prayer of Thankfulness and Blessings

Oh, how I love You, Lord! Thank You for Your kindness, peace, and strength. Lord, I pray for those whom I will connect with today. Please use me to speak encouragement and blessings. God, I pray for our pastors today- Bless them, help them, and give them time to be with You. Guide and lead them according to Your will and purpose.

Help me, Lord, to love more, forgive, and serve You in spite of difficulties. Heal me from past hurts and disappointments. I trust You, Lord; thank You for loving me and being faithful- Even when my heart strayed, You stayed with me, loved, and forgave me, and took care of me. I praise You, Lord!

Prayer of Trust and Thankfulness

Lord, I am so thankful for You. I am excited about Your divine will for my life. I will trust You and follow Your lead. I do not have to know the future because You are my future. Thank You for faith, for loving me so much, and for blessing my loved ones. You are so wonderful! *"He makes my feet like hind's feet, and sets me upon my high places." (Psalm 18:33)*

Lord, thank You for being with me during difficult times, dry places, and even the wilderness. Thank You for the *"times of refreshing that comes from Your Presence" (Acts 3:19-20)* and the oasis (the wellspring of Your love) in the desert.

Great is thy faithfulness; it is new every morning (Lamentations 3:22-26)!

Prayer: Spiritual Weapons

Dear Lord, thank You for revealing that I have been struggling with anger, criticism, and unforgiveness because I have not submitted to Your Word regarding spiritual warfare. When I am attacked (criticized or rejected), I take it personally and blame the person instead of seeing it as a spiritual matter. The Bible clearly teaches us that our struggle is not carnal but spiritual (Ephesians 6:11-13).

And Lord, You assured us that You are the only true Judge, who will vindicate according to Your perfect will (Romans 12:18-20). Forgive me for my self-rule posture and for not dealing with people according to Your Word. Lord, I will not take Your correction lightly.

I renounce the spirit of the carnal nature that tries to exalt itself against the truth of God (2 Corinthians 10:4-6). Thank You for showing me the error of my ways. Thank You for speaking to my heart. I cherish Your leading and Presence. I worship and honor You. How precious is Your name in all the earth? I tremble at the thought of You.

Help me to see through Your spiritual eyes. I refuse to be ruled by carnality. I will lend my soul to righteousness. I turn to You to find grace and mercy (Hebrews 4:16). I resist the enemy and surrender to Your kingdom rule in my life. According to Your Word, it is done.

Prayer to Know You Deeper

It feels so good to walk in the confidence of His grace and to trust the Lord, no matter what happens (Hebrews 4:14-16). I'm excited about being aware of Your Presence. I want to honor You more and be more aware of Your awesome greatness and presence. You are so wonderful. I want to tremble at the thought of You. (Isaiah 66:1-3)

Help me, Lord, to understand You more profoundly, who You are, how much You love me, and how Your love is expressed in my life. Forgive me for my presumptuous (arrogant) sins. Lord, I love You. I magnify and adore You.

You are better than life! (Psalms 63:2-4)

Yes, Lord!

Dear Lord, I am amazed by Your great love for me. When I think about how much You have forgiven me and how much I do not deserve Your grace and mercy, it overwhelms me. I am so sorry for holding things against people and being slow to forgive. I really don't have the right to refuse to forgive. Help me, Lord!

Please cause the power of Your Word to set me free from the bondage of a wounded spirit. There is nothing anyone has done to me that I have not done as well, a thousand times and more. But You continue to forgive me. You sent Your Son, Jesus Christ, to shed His sinless blood for our sake, to forgive us. Even when we were Your enemies, You made provisions for salvation.

Lord, thank You for Your love, grace, and faithfulness towards us. What great love You have for us. I need to continually draw closer to You. I cannot do Your will unless I am connected to the vine, Jesus Christ. I denounce the spirit of my flesh, which is enmity against You. I choose to walk in the newness of life that You have provided. I am a new creature. Old things have passed away, and now I am new. I choose forgiveness, healing, and freedom to say yes to Your will.

Thank You, Father, for helping me...

Quotes from Other Faith Leaders:

A Message on Joy

for the kingdom of God is not eating and drinking, but righteousness and peace and joy in the Holy Spirit. Romans 14:17
...Do not grieve, for the joy of the LORD is your strength" Nehemiah 8:10c.

You make known to me the path of life; in your presence there is fullness of joy; at your right hand are pleasures forevermore. Psalm 16:11

Definitions
" Joy is the fruit of a right relation with God. It is not something people can create by their efforts. The Bible distinguishes joy from pleasure. The Greek word for pleasure is the word from which we get our word *hedonism*, the philosophy of self-centered pleasure-seeking. Paul referred to false teachers as "lovers of pleasures more than lovers of God" 2 Timothy 3:4

Biblical joy comes from the Lord. It is a perpetual gladness of the heart that comes from knowing, experiencing, and trusting Jesus. Martin Lloyd-Jones said, "Joy, in other words, is the response and the reaction of the soul to a knowledge of the Lord Jesus Christ."

We are commanded to be glad, rejoice, and shout for joy. Joy is a deliberate act of obedience in response to who Christ is and what he has done. In happy or sad times, in comfort or difficulty, we find joy in the presence of the Lord. Focusing on Christ-who he is, what he's done to save us, and his promise to keep us-brings a supernatural joy that can't compare with temporary happiness.[lxx]

This 'I' was made in the image of God for fellowship with God. Without God, it is miserable, empty, confused, and frustrated. Without God, life has no meaning, but with God, at its center there is life, inner strength and peace, a deep satisfaction, and unfading joy known only to those who know Jesus Christ.[lxxi]

Rick Warren defined joy: "Joy is the settled assurance that God is in control of all the details of my life, the quiet confidence that ultimately everything is going to be alright and the determined choice to praise God in every situation."

****

- Joy is a gift from God!
- Joy is the fruit of a trusting relationship with God.
- Only Christians can experience true joy.

I am concerned about the lack of joy on the faces of God's people. We seem so heavy and sad these days. I want to know what is going on in your life. Even though the mouth speaks, all is well; our countenance tells a different story. Whatever happened to "**the joy of our salvation**?" I am not referring to brief bursts of joy when we experience something good, but in 1 Peter 1, it says...

> **8** and though you have not seen Him, you love Him, and though you do not see Him now, but believe in Him, you greatly rejoice with joy inexpressible and full of glory, **9** obtaining as the outcome of your faith the salvation of your souls.

The joy that flows out of the vibrant presence of our Lord! Are the "cares of this world" responsible for the lack of joy we experience? Are we too focused on the struggles of this life? Is it too much social media? Do we have too much idle time too many material things, or do we need to accomplish more or be more involved in more activities? Why are you so sad? Is there no satisfaction with having a relationship with God? Where is the glowing presence of the Lord in the faces of believers today?

What happened to the simplicity of faith in Jesus Christ? Have we moved away from the simplicity of pure devotion to Christ?[lxxii] What are we devoted to? Is it riches, status, comfort, the problems of this life and family or a good cause? A good indicator of our devotion is how we spend our time and the focus of our thoughts.

Take a moment to ask yourself, how do I spend my time? Social media, gaming, shopping, reading secular books, church work, activity after activity with the business of life? How much time do you spend reading the Bible, studying a spiritual topic, praying, quiet time, listening to worship music, sharing the gospel, thinking about the goodness of God, resisting ungodly beliefs and thoughts, encouraging saints in the Lord, talking about the goodness of the Lord?

How do you build your faith? As I have come to understand biblical joy, it is clear that joy is the work of the Holy Spirit, and joy comes from having a trusting relationship with Christ. Not just religious activities but a relationship that suggests abiding faith and closeness, like being aware of His presence. Jesus tells us in John 15 that abiding love and obedience brings joy. If we don't live in His love with pure devotion, think about Him and know who we are in Him, our joy cannot be complete.

Several matters impact the degree to which we experience the joy of the Lord. Our relationship with the Lord must include abiding love, hope and obedience. But we also have joy-killers. There are some joy killers, such as not forgiving ourselves and not confessing our sins. **Other joy killers include unhealed hurts and broken hearts, unresolved grief, living in the past, disappointments and failures, past traumas, and generational curses. And finally, that secret struggle of being double-minded!!**

We want all the blessings that come with salvation but not the humility and self-denial that come with having a refreshing, vibrant walk with the Lord. Many times, I just pretended like I was denying myself, but only sometimes. Romans 8:6-13 says to live in the Spirit, we have to "by the Spirit, put to death the misdeeds of the sinful nature." The sinful nature is hostile against God, and it cannot please God. We can try to fool others, but the Lord knows whether we are walking in life or flesh.

Even as believers, if our minds are only concerned about the cares of this world and how to please fallen nature, we have moved from spiritual life to carnal minds. Joy is a product of spiritual life, which is why it is called the **fruit of the Holy Spirit**.[lxxiii]

Our joy is full when we focus on God with faith and devotion (with our whole heart) because He first loved us and lived with Him in truth. This is called the **joy of being with God**.

Furthermore, as we endure suffering and self-sacrifice with a thankful heart, reach the lost, make disciples and bless people, we experience the **joy of doing His will**…which is our "crown of rejoicing" at His coming and knowing that as we suffer with Jesus, we build up an eternal weight of glory in heaven.[lxxiv]

Jesus promised that rivers of living water would flow through us-this living water would be the life of Christ in our hearts (John 7:38). He intended to flow unhindered through us to others. We are so busy "doing" that we never take a moment to "being" a river flowing and blessing others. We are His chosen vessels of honor, set aside for His service-to be ambassadors for Christ. Joy is part of our tool kit for this life. Joy gives us gladness of heart and strength. Joy is a gracious gift from God that helps us do His will as we live in this fallen world!

He wants us to walk with Him, for what purpose? We need to experience His joy as we walk in the understanding of knowing who we are in Jesus Christ and all that comes with belonging to God. Praise God!

Prayer In Closing...

Lord, we come to You in the name of Jesus. We need a refresh from You. We pray God that You would teach us how to walk close to You. And teach us, Lord, how to have a heart condition that longs for Your will. Again, Lord, forgive us for trying to live life our way. We always want to do it our way. But Your way is the path to life. So, God, give us the power to submit to You and to be humble before You. Oh God, when we hear Your name, our hearts will overflow with love for You because You love us with everlasting love. We need a refreshing today, God; we pray in the name of Jesus.

And Lord, we want to know You better. Not just in our minds but in our hearts and souls to know how merciful and wonderful You are and Your willingness to bless us. Lord, we don't always understand the true meaning of eternal blessings. We think blessings are material, but the true blessing is YOU. Our confidence in knowing that You are our Father is the real treasure.

Give us a vibrant prayer life and reveal how to commune with You. Teach us to be devoted to You. Teach us how to walk with You, not run before You or lag behind. But give us the ability to walk with You and be intentional about your kind works and purposes. Help Your people, God. We ask this in the name of Jesus.

We are resolved, and we pray that we will be what You called us to be-Lights in dark places so that You can shine through us, Lord. God, help us to have an answer when someone asks a question about You. God, I ask that You bless and touch us to be vessels of love, kindness, and living water.

In the name of Jesus and for His sake...Amen.

About the Author
Denese S. Brown, Author

Denese is an ordained teacher and associated pastor who serves with her husband, Pastor Roger at Faith Assembly Church in Southeast Michigan. Denese has been a non-profit leader for agencies that aid hurting and disadvantaged families for more than 35 years. She earned an undergraduate degree from Eastern Michigan University, a Master's in social work from the University of Michigan, and completed some coursework at Moody Theological Seminary.

Denese has experienced some difficult times that caused her to cry out to the Lord on many occasions. It was during these painful seasons that her faith was challenged, and her love for God deepened. So often, it was an anointed devotional message or a great book that spoke to her heart and helped her draw closer. Over the years, the Lord has honored her to use many of these lessons to help others grow and connect with the Lord. So, in the same manner that she sensed the Lord giving her direction in His Word, she sensed His prompting to revise this book.

Subsequently, answered prayer encouraged her to share His wisdom as she experienced His abiding love, intimacy, and guidance. Hence, an updated devotional book that includes living proof of His love and promises. The title was inspired by the beautiful, life-giving presence of God's love for His people.

Surely goodness and lovingkindness will follow me all the
days of my life,
And I will dwell in the house of the Lord forever.
Psalms 23:6

References

Choosing Forgiveness by John and Paula Sanford, 1996
Chosen Vessels by Rebecca Osaigbovo, 2002
Discover your God-Given Gifts by Don & Katie Fortune, 1987
Holiness, Truth and the Presence of God by Francis Frangipane, 1986
Intimacy with the Almighty by Charles Swindoll, 1996
Journey into the Divided Heart: Facing the Defense Mechanisms That Hinder True Emotional Healing by Steve Fair © 2019
My Utmost for His Highest by Oswald Chambers, 1935
Needless Casualties of War by John Paul Jackson, 1999
Restoring the Foundations Publication, Third Edition May 2013
Rhythms of Rest by Shelly Miller. Baker Publishing Group. Kindle Edition, pg. 90
The Expository Dictionary of Bible Words by Lawrence Richards, 1985, page 320
The Pursuit of God Legacy Edition, by A.W. Tozer, 1993
The Wiersbe Bible Commentary by Warren W. Wiersbe, 2007
Vines Expository Dictionary of Old and New Testament Words, 1247
According to His Kind Intention - Devotional by Denese Brown, 2015.

[i] 1 Corinthians 13
[ii] 1 John 4:7-8
[iii] Romans 5:6-8
[iv] 1 Peter 4:8
[v] Holiness, Truth and the Presence of God by Francis Frangipane, 1986
[vi] Holiness, Truth and the Presence of God by Francis Frangipane, 1986
[vii] John 4:23-24
[viii] John 8:32
[ix] Vines Expository Dictionary of Old and New Testament Words, 1247
[x] Romans 12:1
[xi] Matthew 5:8
[xii] Acts 3:19
[xiii] Isa. 66:2
[xiv] Duet 30:6
[xv] Isa. 66:1-2
[xvi] Philippians 3:3 (Worship the Lord)

[xvii] The Expository Dictionary of Bible Words by Lawrence Richards 1985, page 320 (Grace Apprehended)
[xviii] 2 Corinthians 12:9
[xix] 2 Corinthians 9:6-8
[xx] Malachi 3:10-12
[xxi] 2 Corinthians 2:9 (The River of Giving)
[xxii] Chosen Vessels by Rebecca Osaigbovo, 2002
[xxiii] Ephesians 3:20
[xxiv] 1 Corinthians 2:9
[xxv] My Utmost for His Highest by Oswald Chambers, 1935
[xxvi] Romans 8:28-29 (Joy in Trials)
[xxvii] Matthews 11:28-30, The Message
[xxviii] 2 Corinthians 10:4
[xxix] John 15:5 (Rhythms of Grace)

[xxx] Restoring the Foundations Publication, Third Edition May 2013
[xxxi] Choosing Forgiveness by John and Paula Sanford, 1996
[xxxii] Genesis 3:8 (Be Available)

[xxxiii] Building on the Atonement by Oswald Chambers, October 9th (Rest In His Power)
[xxxiv] Psalms 139:6
[xxxv] 1 John 1:9

[xxxvi] Jas 1:17
[xxxvii] Psalm 119:2
[xxxviii] Philippians 2
[xxxix] Proverb 15:31-33 (The Mind of Christ)

[xl] Psalm 46, 50
Psalm 59, 60
Psalm 19
Genesis 39:1-23
1Corthians 2:14-3:15
Mark 2:1-12 (Great I Am)

[xli] Miller, Shelly. Rhythms of Rest (p. 90-1). Baker Publishing Group. Kindle Edition. (God's Rest)

[xlii] Discover your God-Given Gifts by Don & Katie Fortune, 1987
[xliii] Journey into the Divided Heart: Facing the Defense Mechanisms That Hinder True Emotional Healing © 2019 Steve Fair - Revised Edition
[xliv] According to His Kind Intention - Devotional by Denese Brown. 2015. (God's Message for Life)

[xlv] 2 Corinthians 10:4
[xlvi] Philippians 1:6
[xlvii] Romans 8:37
[xlviii] Needless Casualties of War by John Paul Jackson, 1999
[xlix] Philippians 4:13
[l] John 15:4
[li] 2 Corinthians 10:5
[lii] Philippians 4:7
[liii] Philippians 2
[liv] 2 Corinthians 12:9 (Resist Evil -Warfare is Essential)

[lv] James 4:7-8
[lvi] Romans 12:1
[lvii] Matthews 5:23-24 (What Hinders Your Prayers?)

[lviii] John 15:5
[lix] Romans 8:26-27
[lx] Hebrews 4:16
[lxi] Romans 5:10
[lxii] Romans 3:23

[lxiii] Psalms 15:4
[lxiv] Psalms 139:6
[lxv] John 10:4-5
[lxvi] John 1:4
[lxvii] Lamentations 3:25-26
[lxviii] 1 Corinthians 2:9 (We Must Pray)

[lxix] Intimacy with the Almighty by Charles Swindoll, 1996

[lxx] Nivine Richie
[lxxi] Billy Graham
[lxxii] 2 Corinthians 11:3
[lxxiii] Galatians 5:22
[lxxiv] Thessalonians 2:19-20 (A Message on Joy II)

www.ingramcontent.com/pod-product-compliance
Lightning Source LLC
Chambersburg PA
CBHW052031030426
42337CB00027B/4946